GOOD ∗ OLD ∗ DAYS®

Cooking Up a STORM

Edited by Ken and Janice Tate

HOUSE of
WHITE
BIRCHES
PUBLISHERS
SINCE 1947

Cooking Up a Storm™

Editors: Ken and Janice Tate
Managing Editor: Barb Sprunger
Editorial Assistant: Joanne Neuenschwander
Copy Supervisor: Michelle Beck
Copy Editors: Läna Schurb, Mary O'Donnell

Publishing Services Manager: Brenda Gallmeyer
Art Director: Brad Snow
Assistant Art Director: Nick Pierce
Graphic Arts Supervisor: Ronda Bechinski
Production Artists: Erin Augsburger, Janice Tate
Production Assistants: Cheryl Kempf, Marj Morgan, Judy Neuenschwander, Jessica Tate
Photography: Tammy Christian, Don Clark, Matthew Owen, Jackie Schaffel
Photo Stylists: Tammy Nussbaum, Tammy M. Smith

Publishing Director: David McKee
Marketing Director: Dan Fink
Editorial Director: Gary Richardson

Printed in China
First Printing: 2006
Library of Congress Number: 2005931525
ISBN-10: 1-59217-101-X
ISBN-13: 978-1-59217-101-9

Good Old Days Customer Service: (800) 829-5865

1 2 3 4 5 6 7 8 9

Dear Friends of the Good Old Days,

I have been sharing my memories with readers of *Good Old Days* magazine for over 15 years now, and I'm always amazed at what evokes reminiscences of those happy days that made up my childhood.

Sometimes it can be sight, sound or touch that snaps me back in time. An old photograph reminds me of my childhood home. A tune on the radio carries me back to when my dear wife, Janice, and I were dating decades ago. Or the gentle brush of a velvety petal plants me in Mama's flower garden, caught for the umpteenth time treading on her pansies. And, at least for the moment, I am young again, ready to take on the world.

So it was no surprise when Janice and I began preparation of this special book that my senses of taste and smell would likewise flood my mind with memories of the Good Old Days.

Do you remember the sweet scent of cookies cooling on the table greeted you at the door?

How about the heavenly smell of fresh-baked bread wafting from the kitchen window, just begging to be slathered with butter and jelly for a scrumptious treat after school?

Don't your taste buds nearly burst when you remember the ambrosia of Mama's Sunday chicken dinner!

Those are the memories that are the inspiration for our monthly magazine feature, Good Old Days in the Kitchen, where hundreds of *Good Old Days* readers have shared their stories of home and hearth. The feature consistently has been the most popular feature in our magazine. Why? Because the kitchen was the center of the home and our mothers were the center of our universe.

As an example, our little Ozark Mountain home had three rooms. Mama's kitchen was literally in the center of the house, situated between the living room and the bedroom.

There we ate all of our meals together. Sometimes those meals were only cornbread and buttermilk for dinner or beans for supper, but whatever Daddy provided and Mama cooked in those tough times we were thankful to have. At the same table we gathered to share the day's successes and challenges. The table also served as a desk for homework and a platform for games on rainy days.

So life literally revolved around the kitchen and the woman who spent so much of *her* life in there, cooking up a storm.

The stories and recipes in this book, are some of the best our readers have shared with us through the years. Janice and I hope that, as you read them, you are taken back to your own memories of Mama and her kitchen.

Come on in. The cocoa is hot and the cookies are done. Join us for a look back to the Good Old Days; we'll be Cooking Up a Storm.

Ken Tate

❧ Contents ❧

Delightful Desserts • 98

Supper Around the Table • 130

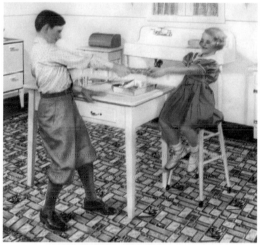

The Most Important Meal

Chapter One

Good days always seem to begin with good breakfasts, and no one could whip up the most important meal of the day the way Mama could. Whether it was eggs and bacon, pancakes and sausage, or just a steaming bowl of oatmeal, she seemed to know exactly what her growing brood needed before tramping out the door for school.

I was a bit balky at times when it came to the morning meal, but Mama always insisted on two things: First, we had to gather at the table for breakfast together unless it was just flatly impossible. Second, we had to eat breakfast because, as she said, "It's the most important meal of the day."

Being the balky one, usually arriving bleary-eyed at the table, and a notoriously slow eater anyway, I always seemed to be the one holding up the assembly-line preparation for school.

"I don't care if you are running late," she admonished me. "Chew your food— don't gulp. And be sure to finish your milk!"

Then it was off to face the day. In winter, Mama made sure we were bundled up to brave snow and wind. In spring and autumn, the final preparation was less rushed since we had a few less layers to deal with. But the most important layer of protection was a delicious, hot and wholesome morning meal.

"Chew your food—don't gulp. And be sure to finish your milk!"

In today's harried lifestyles, breakfast has become a forgotten art. More often than not, children leave for school without eating anything at all, or with only some fast-food, nutritionally-deprived substitute. Most schools have breakfast programs for underprivileged youngsters.

Back when I was a young sprout, I considered any child underprivileged who left for school without a good breakfast.

I still like to eat a big breakfast today— I just can't eat nearly as large a portion as I once did. Probably my favorite breakfast now is when my dear wife Janice prepares her corned-beef hash and eggs. But whether it's eggs, pancakes, waffles or hot cereal, she knows how much I need a good breakfast.

After all, as Mama used to say, it's the most important meal of the day.

—*Ken Tate*

Corned-Beef Hash & Eggs

Preheat oven to 350 degrees.
- 15 ounces corned-beef hash
- 4 eggs
- Salt and pepper
- Vegetable cooking oil

Divide corned-beef hash evenly into four 7-ounce ovenproof oiled serving dishes. With a spoon, press corned-beef hash up sides to make a "cup" in each of the dishes. Crack an egg, either scrambled or sunny-side up, into each dish. Sprinkle lightly with salt and pepper.

Bake in preheated oven for 20 minutes or until eggs reach desired firmness. Remove and allow to cool 5 minutes before serving in dish.

Note: You may add your own toppings to the finished dish. Cheese, cayenne pepper, salsa or sour cream are among our favorites.

Oatmeal Versus Cream of Wheat

By Helen Bolterman

When I was a youngster in the 1930s and early 1940s, during the Depression era, families did without luxuries, including extra money for household groceries. The large, two-story house our family rented in La Crosse, Wis., had a big yard and a good-sized garden. That garden provided many vegetables for our family meals. Mother also canned many of its offerings to eat later, during the long winter months.

Menus for our family of seven were quite simple. On cold winter mornings, breakfast consisted mainly of hot cooked oatmeal or Cream of Wheat; otherwise, cold cereal was the usual offering. Modern groceries offer many brands of boxed cereal, including the colorful, sugar-coated varieties preferred by some of today's youngsters. Back then, however, our family had a choice of corn flakes, puffed wheat (which came in large, family-size bags) or shredded-wheat biscuits.

I detested oatmeal; I thought it was thick, lumpy and unappetizing. And even when I added a good scoop of sugar, it didn't taste palatable. I preferred Cream of Wheat. When there was leftover Cream of Wheat, Mother would fry it the next day and serve it with delicious syrup. I considered that a real treat.

Much of the fruit our family ate came in the form of large sacks of grapefruit received from a government surplus fund. Prunes were also commonly served for breakfast in our household. Oranges and bananas, on the other hand, were treats, and we children relished them on those rare occasions when our family could afford them.

We purchased our milk at a neighborhood milk station. Customers were required to furnish their own containers; we used tin syrup buckets that Mother carefully washed.

Father did our grocery shopping at a small neighborhood store. Soup meat and liver were cheap and so they often formed the basis for our evening meals. The grocers allowed our father to charge groceries, and when Dad paid the bill, the owner would throw in a few candy bars for us children. Also, since our family included a cat—Nebby, the house mouser—they would throw in a free kidney for the kitty.

Mother used the garden vegetables when she cooked a large kettle of soup for our family of seven. I loved Mother's homemade soup.

Facing page: 1937 Cream of Wheat ad, House of White Birches nostalgia archives

The "Champ"

—he needs your help, mother!

GIVE HIM PLENTY OF THIS VITAL FOOD ENERGY EVERY DAY

The "champ" to his playmates... but you know, mother, he is still a very little chap who burns up each day more bodily energy in proportion to his size than a grown-up.

Breakfasts are supremely vital now. For he gets up in the morning with his energy supply at a low point. His system calls for, craves, demands food energy to help him face the tremendously active hours just ahead.

Delicious Cream of Wheat will help supply abundantly that daily food energy . . . and will release it for use speedily, without burdening even delicate digestions.

Join the millions whose children have thrived on Cream of Wheat during the past 42 years!

Sticks to the ribs! Young systems crave nourishment like this. Cream of Wheat offers carbohydrate for quick food energy, protein for muscle building. Yet it is digested with ease. Digestion begins right in the mouth!

Quick food energy of the sort your own doctor will tell you your child needs for activity and growth. This famous hot cereal provides it abundantly. As part of an adequate diet, it also helps stimulate steady, natural weight gains.

CREAM OF WHEAT

IMPORTANT: The Council on Foods of the American Medical Association has awarded to Cream of Wheat the "Seal of Acceptance". This officially indicates that this famous hot cereal and the advertising for it are acceptable to the Council.

Less than ½ cent a serving is the low cost of Cream of Wheat. This cereal cooks up to 6 times its original volume, so that each package yields over 50 generous helpings. It pays to make Cream of Wheat your family breakfast cereal!

3½ million bowls served daily! That's how youngsters love delicious, steaming hot Cream of Wheat. Only the best hard wheat from leading growing areas —heat-treated, purified and blended—can yield such matchless flavor. Order Cream of Wheat today. It's quick and simple to prepare.

1925 Quaker Puffed Wheat and Rice ad, House of White Birches nostalgia archives

I had a harder time with the frequent meals of steamed liver that she smothered in onions (which I also didn't relish). I usually attempted to hide bits of liver around and under my plate, but I was frequently caught in the act.

We were expected to eat whatever was put on our plates. Refusal to do so could mean no supper at all, or a trip directly to bed.

Another favorite meal of mine was sauerkraut and spare ribs. I particularly loved to feast on the soft, chewy bones. Today we can purchase the meatier country ribs, but I still enjoy the taste of the sweeter spare ribs.

Canned vegetables were rare in our house, but we stretched them when we had them. Canned peas were prepared as creamed peas, making a larger vegetable offering to feed our

household. I still make them once in a while. My husband, Wes, gets a hankering for them occasionally when he remembers the creamed peas his mother made during his youth.

The iceman worked regular routes to deliver chunks of ice to families with iceboxes. We children loved to see him coming. We knew that we could gather ice chips from his wagon for Mother to make ice-cold lemonade. It wasn't until the late 1930s or early 1940s that our family purchased our first electric refrigerator.

Desserts were always special treats. When cake was served, we five children always kept a close watch on the seven slices on the serving plate, and raced to finish our meals so that we could grab the biggest piece first. Tapioca and bread puddings were also favorites, and who could forget Mom's delicious custard pie?

Though we lived frugally during the Depression years, our parents always provided good, nourishing food. As an added health measure, our mother always saw to it that we took cod liver oil to protect us from the nasty viruses that were so prevalent during the cold winter months. We swallowed that tablespoonful of oil reluctantly indeed. Perhaps Mother was right, though; aren't fish and fish oils recommended today as great health foods?

After Wes and I married, I learned to cook liver and onions, too. I even discovered that I *liked* it when I fried the meat in bacon drippings until crispy instead of steaming it, as Mother did.

But to this day, the only way I can eat oatmeal is in cookies—and my favorite hot cereal is *still* Cream of Wheat. ❖

The Griswold Skillet

By Winnie Schuetz

I have a very precious possession that has been in my family since many years before I was born. Sometime in the early 1920s, while my father was working for a hardware company in Rockford, Ill., he special-ordered a No.12 Griswold skillet with a self-basting cover. It turned out to be one of the best buys he ever made.

How can I describe all the wonderful things that were produced in that skillet? Two of my all-time favorites were Mom's fried chicken and Father's chicken fricassee. He was a fine and experimental cook. If you have never had chicken fricassee, you have missed a great culinary treat. A close second was pork liver and onions. I've never had better liver and onions anywhere; I believe it has to be that self-basting cover.

After Mom passed away when I was 16, my father continued to cook for the two of us and any young men who came courting. I have always wondered if my husband fell in love with me or with the delectable victuals that came from that skillet.

After I married, Father continued to cook tasty meals in the big old skillet for company and for my family when we visited. Finally, one day when he came for a visit, he brought me the skillet and said I had more use for it than he did. Now it was mine.

He gave me careful instructions on its care. To maintain a cast-iron skillet so that food doesn't stick, you must never wash it with soap. Actually, washing is seldom necessary; a quick wipe-out with a pot rag usually does the job. After making gravy or fricassee, put hot water in the skillet for 15 minutes and then wipe out the residue; that takes care of most things.

If, at some point, things begin to stick, then it is time to reseason the skillet. Simply rub the inside of the skillet with lard or a good vegetable shortening and place it in a very slow oven (set on the lowest temperature) and leave it in the oven for two or three hours. Wipe the skillet with a dry rag or paper towels, and it is ready to use again.

That old Griswold skillet has made a big impression in our family. One year my daughter-in-law wanted a skillet like mine for Christmas. Despite a diligent search, I couldn't find one. I had to settle for one sold in a store that carries Amish utensils. The lid was sold separately and probably cost 10 times what mine cost.

These days I live alone, since my lifetime partner of almost 49 years went home to the Lord. Every time I use the skillet, I wish I could make fried chicken once more for him.

My youngest son, John, always wants me to make fried chicken for his birthday. I usually do. He loves to cook like his granddad did, and I think that I will ask him to use the big skillet to make fried chicken for *me* on my next birthday. Maybe he will be the guardian of the big skillet for his generation.

Being the caretaker of such an old treasure is a great responsibility.

I find it amazing that such a simple, uncomplicated thing like a skillet can serve several generations for more than 80 years, and still do it like it did when Father first got it. What other piece of kitchen equipment will last that long, much less hold the enthusiasm of subsequent generations? It just goes to show that oldies are still goodies! ❖

Grandma's Biscuits

By Jeanne C. Shirley

Hot biscuits are favorite breakfast fare for me and my family, but few compare with Grandma's biscuits. Those luscious morsels entered my life back when cholesterol, television programs and space flights were not part of the conversation at most social gatherings.

Grandma's biscuits set the standard, making today's canned variety totally unacceptable. Like hers, the biscuits for my family are "made from scratch." In Grandma's day and time, it was the only way.

Up before sunrise, she pumped up the old bottled-gas range and dug in. Yes, dug in. Grandma's biscuits were done by hand, hands washed and wiped half-dry on the apron tied around her ample waist. The wide, gold wedding band, her only jewelry, was placed securely in the free-standing cupboard.

This cupboard featured a flour bin suspended over the work area. By turning a small handle, Grandma sifted a mound of flour into the large wooden bowl that waited below. She possessed two of these hand-smoothed, gleaming bowls, both used for mixing dough in a bed of dry flour. For breakfast biscuits, the larger bowl was needed.

> *Like hers, the biscuits for my family were "made from scratch."*

First, Grandma made a small indentation in the heap of flour. Her quick, sure fingers scooped salt from the open glass salt "cellar" suspended inside the cupboard door, which enclosed the flour bin and other baking supplies. Her fingers "measured" the baking soda, and the dollop of lard slipped into each of several pie tins, encrusted and blackened from daily use in the biscuit making.

She gave no thought to cholesterol as a lump of animal fat was swiftly worked into the hill of flour. Her fingers squeezed and spread, squeezed and spread, just until the mixture reached the right consistency. Then she scooped a new indentation in the flour mixture to receive a splash of buttermilk, complete with the glob of starter, stored from yesterday.

After gentle mixing, she lifted the soft mass from its bed of unused, untouched flour and plopped, flopped and folded it onto the flour-covered cupboard top.

Satisfied that it had reached the texture for fluffy biscuits, she patted the mass into a thin circle. Grandma specialized in the crisp kind; she never made thick, doughy biscuits. The top of a drinking glass was dipped into flour and pressed into the soft dough, making a myriad of small circles.

"Biscuits are about ready," rang out as Grandma pulled the warmed biscuit pans from the hot oven.

Did she ever burn her fingers as she gave each morsel of soft dough a quick *swish, swish* to coat both top and bottom with fat, heated just below the smoking level? Back to the oven went the filled pans, and the family had better gather—or be left out.

I liked winter visits best, with breakfast by the soft glow of the coal-oil lamp. Cousins, shoved together on a long bench behind the table, experienced a happy and very satisfying breakfast. A glass of cold milk, a large bowl of oatmeal topped with cream from the family cows and, of course, biscuits, greeted us each morning.

There was never any question about "What's for breakfast?" It was standard fare. No diets, no worry about cholesterol—and no lounging in bed, or you'd miss out.

Yes, I wanted my biscuits hot, hot enough to melt home-churned butter through every flake, right down to the golden-brown crust. And that crust had to be crisp enough to crunch quietly as, with butter-stained fingers, I consumed Grandma's prize biscuits.

The first biscuit, lavishly buttered, was eaten with the oatmeal. The next was sometimes spread with a thin layer of honey or jelly.

If more family were home, we'd have fried bacon or ham and a large cast-iron skillet full of gravy. But what I remember best is two biscuit halves, thin and slightly crisp, golden with butter.

Cholesterol? We didn't know anything about that. Did the daily dose of oatmeal keep everything in balance? Did our cows and pigs not produce cholesterol?

In her late 70s, Grandma quit making biscuits. "It's no fun now that I'm alone." In her 80s she said, "I'm too tired." By her 90s she had no kitchen.

Her daughters and granddaughters make a pretty good biscuit, but something is missing—Grandma's magic touch.

I look at my "no-cholesterol vegetable shortening," the "lite" margarine, the cultured buttermilk. Is that where the magic has gone? Does my family really think my biscuits are special? Is it the love shared when family gathers that gives us memories to treasure? ❖

Breakfast & Biscuits

By Betty Jane Atkinson

*L*ooking back to my childhood, I now realize the work Mamma had to do to keep her family of nine fed and clean. Every morning, rain or shine, Mamma was up at daylight to make biscuits. I would wake to the sound of her shaking down the ashes from the firebox of the wood-burning stove. A good roaring fire was needed to heat the oven to 400 degrees.

Mamma made her famous biscuits at the kitchen cabinet. She slid out the granite top of the cabinet to work on and sprinkled flour on its wiped-clean surface. Her mixing bowl was a deep stone crockery bowl. The dough was worked by hand until it was dumped onto the floured place.

Using her hands, Mamma rolled the edges toward the middle and patted the dough out to roll the edges in again and again, her fingertips pressing not too gently into the folded dough until it felt right. She then patted the dough into a flattened circle as thick as her finger. I never saw her use a rolling pin to flatten the

Buttermilk Biscuits

Preheat oven to 450 degrees.
Sift together:
- 1¾ cups flour
- ½ teaspoon salt
- 2 teaspoons baking powder
- 1 teaspoon sugar
- ½ teaspoon baking soda

Cut in:
- 5 tablespoons butter or ¼ cup lard

Add and lightly mix (25 strokes only):
- ¾ cup buttermilk or ¾ cup sweet milk mixed with with 1 tablespoon vinegar

Turn dough onto floured board and knead gently for 30 seconds. Pat dough to a thickness of ¼ inch. Cut with biscuit cutter. Bake on ungreased cookie sheet for 10 to 12 minutes.

Note: It is best to stack two cookie sheets, one on top of the other, to prevent over-browning the biscuit bottoms.

dough. She used a tin can to cut the biscuits.

When I was growing up as the eldest of eight, Mamma made three dozen biscuits every morning, seven days a week. Any leftover from breakfast were eaten later in the day. The baby would hold a cold biscuit and sit quietly for a long while, nibbling on it.

Mamma only took a vacation from making biscuits when she had a new baby. After the last baby she never had a vacation. Once I figured out how many biscuits she made in my 15 years. Since she took few vacations, I figured she had made more than 13,000. And she continued making them long after I left home.

One by one, Mamma's kids grew up, married and went to their own homes. She continued to make biscuits every morning, but not so many. If someone dropped by, they could always find a cold biscuit to eat with a dab of jelly on it.

Then Daddy had a fatal stroke, and suddenly Mamma was alone with no one to make biscuits for. Mamma came to live with me. When I asked if she would like to make us some biscuits, she said, "No kitchen should have two cooks. I have retired."

When I asked for her biscuit recipe, she was willing to give it to me. She said I was to take a couple or so handsful of flour, a dash of salt, a little soda, a bit of lard and some buttermilk from churning. Mix it all up, and that was it!

I followed as best I could, mixing and kneading as I had seen her do. They looked so fluffy and white as I turned them into the warm shortening in an iron skillet. I thought they would be as good as Mamma's. But when I took them out of my gas oven they had a hard, dark brown crust—not a soft, golden crust like Mamma's. And the insides were heavy; Mamma's were always light as a feather. Mamma said she had no secret in making her biscuits; she just had a lot of practice.

We have a family reunion every year and Mamma's buttermilk biscuits are always remembered. We all agree that no one can make a biscuit to equal Mamma's. Mamma sits and grins and says, "Shoot, they weren't that good!" But we all know they were *better* then good and would have taken blue ribbons in any contest. ❖

Grape Sunshine

By Jeanne Boberg

This recipe is handwritten in my mother's spiral-bound canning notebook. I first remember it from the winter day when my Aunt Inez spread the rich purple on slices of warm, buttered toast and carried them to the rocker near the kitchen window. "This is grape sunshine," she said as we snuggled down together. The skies were cold and gray outside, but the sweet treat gleamed with the past summer's warmth and sun. ❖

Grape Sunshine

5 pounds Concord grapes
3 pounds sugar

Wash grapes carefully and remove from stems. Weigh, and to each 5 pounds of grapes add 3 pounds of sugar. Do not add water. Boil carefully for 40–50 minutes.

Cool and run through a colander. Reheat and can.

One book that tells how to safely can fruit butters is the *Ball Blue Book*. Information can be obtained by writing: Ball Corp., Consumer Products Division, 345 S. High St., Muncie, IN 47305-2326.

Marvelous Muffins

uffins—like biscuits—were a staple of the staple of the American breakfast table back in the Good Old Days. Reader Kay Barnes submitted these recipes for marvelous muffins from clippings she had saved for over 50 years. *Bon appetit!* ❖

Perfect Muffins

2 cups sifted flour
¼ cup sugar
3 teaspoons baking powder
½ teaspoon salt
1 cup milk
⅓ cup vegetable oil or melted shortening
1 egg

Preheat oven to 400 degrees. Grease bottoms of 14 (2½-inch) muffin pan-cups or 11 (3-inch) muffin-pan cups; or line cups with paper liners.

Sift together flour, sugar, baking powder and salt into large bowl; set

aside. Combine milk, oil and egg; blend with fork to mix well. Make a well in center of flour mixture. Pour in milk mixture all at once and stir quickly with fork, just until flour disappears. Do not beat; batter will be lumpy.

Quickly spoon or pour batter into muffin cups, filling them slightly more than half-full. Spoon only once for each cup.

Bake for 20 to 25 minutes, or until golden and cake tester inserted in center comes out clean. Loosen edges of muffins with spatula; turn out. Serve hot. Makes 11 or 14.

Blueberry Muffins

Make Perfect Muffins (above), increasing sugar to ⅓ cup. Add 1 cup fresh blueberries, washed and well-drained, or ¾ cup well-drained canned or thawed frozen blueberries, to dry ingredients. Proceed as directed.

Fill 2½-inch muffin-pan cups. Lightly sprinkle with sugar. Bake as directed. Makes 16 to 18.

Raisin Muffins

Make Perfect Muffins (facing page), adding 1 tablespoon grated orange peel and ½ cup seedless raisins to dry ingredients. Proceed as directed.

Fill 2½-inch muffin-pan cups. Bake as directed. Makes 14 to 16.

Strawberry Jam Muffins

Make Perfect Muffins (facing page), adding 1 teaspoon grated lemon peel to dry ingredients. Proceed as directed.

Put 1 tablespoon batter in each 2½-inch muffin-pan cup. Add 1 teaspoon strawberry jam to each. Add enough batter to fill cups two-thirds full. Bake as directed. Makes 14.

Cheese Muffins

Make Perfect Muffins (facing page), adding ½ cup grated sharp Cheddar cheese and ¼ teaspoon dry mustard to dry ingredients, and reducing oil or melted shortening to ¼ cup and sugar to 3 tablespoons. Proceed as directed.

Fill 2½-inch muffin-pan cups. Bake as directed. Makes 14 to 16.

Orange-Walnut Muffins

Make Perfect Muffins (facing page), adding 2 tablespoons grated orange peel and ⅓ cup coarsely chopped walnuts to dry ingredients.

Proceed as directed. Fill 2½-inch muffin-pan cups. Bake as directed. Makes 14 to 16.

Bacon Muffins

Make Perfect Muffins (facing page), adding ½ cup coarsely chopped, crisp, cooked bacon to dry ingredients, and reducing oil or melted shortening to ¼ cup. Proceed as directed.

Fill 2½-inch muffin-pan cups. Bake as directed. Makes 14 to 16.

Buttermilk Muffins

Make Perfect Muffins (facing page), reducing baking powder to 2 teaspoons and adding ½ teaspoon baking soda to dry ingredients; substitute an equal amount of buttermilk for milk. Proceed as directed. Fill 2½-inch muffin-pan cups. Bake as directed. Makes 14 to 16.

Corn Muffins

1 cup sifted flour
¼ cup sugar
3 teaspoons baking powder
½ teaspoon salt
1 cup yellow cornmeal
1 cup milk
⅓ cup vegetable oil
1 egg, slightly beaten

Preheat oven to 425 degrees. Grease bottoms of (2½-inch) muffin-pan cups.

Sift together flour, sugar, baking powder and salt into large bowl; set aside.

Combine milk, oil and egg; blend with fork to mix well. Make a well in center of flour mixture. Pour in milk mixture all at once and stir quickly with fork, just until flour disappears. Do not beat; batter will be lumpy.

Quickly spoon or pour batter into muffin cups, filling them not quite two-thirds full. Bake for 15 minutes, or until golden. Loosen edges of muffins with spatula; turn out. Serve warm. Makes 14.

Granny's Advice

By Ann Casper
as told to Jeannie Moore

Back in the 1930s, Granny's advice was the closest thing to psychotherapy. Many considered her a second mother. She was a teacher and friend, and many considered her "the lady with style." People from all over Nowata County came to tell her their problems with marriage, money, cooking, etc. And Granny was loving and kind to all of them.

The ladies gathered in the living room as they collected pieces of material to quilt. Often scraps of fabric from old clothing were cut into

designs and the ladies worked together to make them into a quilt. Sometimes Granny helped some of the women sew. Granny did not use store-bought patterns, but made her own patterns out of old clothing.

I remember her trying to teach me to make a shirt. She helped me cut the pieces of the shirt and tried to show me how to sew them together. I admit that I was a slow learner. I hated sewing, but I tried to pretend that I was interested. Little by little she taught me to sew each piece until the shirt was finished.

Granny often taught women to make clothes for themselves, their children and sometimes their menfolk.

Granny was known for her canning skills, too. Whole families gathered corn, cantaloupe, watermelon, green beans, peas and other vegetables. There were always lots of green onions. I loved eating the stems of the onions.

This time of year, neighbors helped each other. One day they worked in one person's garden and the next day they gathered in ours, and so on.

Once the produce had been harvested, it was time to can. Several women came to Granny to ask how to can different fruits and vegetables. Granny was considered the expert. Granny and I gathered all the jars for canning and put them in a big pan to boil. Sometimes we worked way into the night to finish canning. But Granny never seemed to get tired.

I loved to watch her visit and chat with neighbors as she canned. Where she got her energy, I'll never know, but she never seemed to be tired or cranky. She had a nice word to say about everybody. She said, "If you can't say something nice, don't open your mouth." I can still hear her say that sometimes when I get out of sorts. Many of our modern conveniences weren't available back then. Imagine walking to an outdoor bathroom in the middle of the night. Everyone drank from a big old bucket of water with a dipper. But back then, Granny never mentioned germs.

Granny was a teacher, counselor, friend and second mother to many of the ladies in our county. The neighbors came from all around to chat with her and learn various skills. ❖

Granny's Strawberry Jam
One of Granny's specialties was strawberry jam. Here's the recipe:

6 pints strawberries
1⅓ cups pectin

3 cups sugar
Juice of 1 lemon

Begin by sterilizing the jars. Thoroughly wash and rinse them. Place them in a big pan and boil for approximately 5 minutes. Put lids in small pan and boil for 5 to 10 minutes. Keep lids hot by covering until ready for them.

Thoroughly wash strawberries. Remove stems and trim any bad spots. Mash strawberries until crushed. Place berries, sugar and lemon juice in large kottle (stainless steel is recommended nowadays) and mix. Pour in the pectin when the berries are boiling. Bring berry mixture to a full, rolling boil, then reduce heat and let simmer for approximately 20 to 25 minutes, stirring occasionally so mixture does not stick.

Pour the mixture into 8 to 10 hot sterilized jars, filling to approximately ½ inch from the top. Clean the mouth of the jar and screw on a hot lid with the metal ring tight. Process jars in a hot-water bath for almost 5 minutes.

Carefully remove the jars and place on a clean kitchen towel until they are cool.

Always test the seals. Retighten rings as necessary. Store in a cool, dry place. Let jam age for 2 to 3 weeks before using it.

Jean's Jam

By Nancy Strasser

*I*t was supposed to be *peach* jam … but anyone can make a mistake. It was our first year in a house with a full-size peach tree in the yard, and we were up to our elbows in peaches. We had already tried peach cake, peach rolls and peach ice cream; but it was clear that we weren't going to use up all those peaches while they were fresh. There was nothing left to do but make some preserves.

So Mom got out her canning jars and bought sugar in 20-pound sacks. We spent the last week of August trying every recipe we could find: peach slices, peach jelly and peach butter.

But the adventure of the summer came with the peach jam.

When Mom made anything, she made it in *quantity*. With a jam-eating brood of five (and with bushels of free peaches in the cellar), she scaled her recipe to make 36 pints of preserves. Restaurant-size cooking pots crowded every burner of the stove; pint jars covered every inch of the kitchen counters; peach pits filled the sink; and utensils covered the table.

The kitchen became an assembly line. Eight-year-old Jean hauled peaches from the cellar, while Kathy and I, seasoned veterans around the kitchen at ages 9 and 10, peeled and sliced.

I wouldn't be surprised to find a jar still lurking in the cupboard.

As fast as we poured peach slices into the grinder, Mom turned out purée into a mixing bowl the size of a laundry basket. Mom then added sugar and preservatives, and poured the whole batch into a huge pot on the stove.

Anybody not helping was *not* welcome in the kitchen. But after a full day of processing jam, we all tired of our duties. Jean was caught loafing, so Mom assigned her an additional task: measure out ¼ cup of lemon juice, and add it to the purée.

With all the large bowls and industrial-size utensils on the kitchen table, it's no surprise that Jean misunderstood the quantity to be a "quart" instead of a "quarter cup." Jean didn't need to ask anybody how much 1 quart was; she dutifully measured out 4 cups of lemon juice and poured the juice into with the purée. Unaware of the error, we cooked up that batch of jam, ladled it into jars, and sealed the containers with paraffin.

We started on the next batch of jam before Mom noticed the lemon juice bottle.

"What happened to all the lemon juice? I had a full bottle here!"

Well, it didn't take long to put two and two together: All we had to do was taste the jam residue in the pot. Talk about sour! Mom looked at the 12 sealed jars of peach lemon preserves, and wondered what to do. Throwing it away was not an option; there were 8 cups of costly sugar in those preserves, even if there were plenty more peaches in the basement.

We ended up putting those 12 jars on the shelf with all the other peach products (discreetly labeled "Jean's Jam," so we wouldn't accidentally give it away to unsuspecting friends or neighbors). The next time Mom recruited Kathy, Jean and me to help make preserves, she kept a close eye on her ingredients.

We never had a recurrence of the Jean's Jam fiasco. It's a good thing, too. It took *years* to use up that one batch.

And I wouldn't be surprised to find one or two jars still lurking in the back of Mom's cupboard, even today. ❖

Peach Preserves

10 cups peach purée
¼ cup lemon juice
½ cup powdered fruit pectin
8 cups sugar
Melted paraffin

In saucepan, combine peach purée and lemon juice. Cover and cook over high heat for 2 minutes.

Stir in fruit pectin and, stirring constantly, bring to a rolling boil. Boil and stir for 1 minute. Add sugar. Stirring constantly, bring back to a rolling boil. Boil and stir for 1 minute.

Remove preserves from heat; skim off foam. Fill sterilized jars and seal with ⅛ inch melted paraffin. Cover with metal lids. Makes 12 8-ounce jars.

Heavenly Jam
I am 88 years old and remember my mother making this jam many years ago.

8 pounds Concord grapes
1 box seedless raisins
3 oranges
8 cups sugar

Peal oranges and put them through a fine chopper. Use the juice and orange. Pulp grapes and mash through a sieve. Cook all ingredients together until thick.
—*Mrs. G.L. Wamsley*

An Apple a Day

Submitted by Jeanne Boberg

There is an old saying: An apple a day keeps the doctor away. Nothing was more important back in the Good Old Days than keeping the doctor away, so apples tended to be a staple in our diet. That always reminds me of the poem "Picking the Apples" that I read in the October 1923 issue of *Normal Instructor and Primary Plans* magazine.

Picking the Apples

Apples to pick! Apples to pick!
Come with a basket and come with a stick.
Rustle the trees and shake them down,
And let every boy take care of his crown.
There you go, Tommy! Up with you, Jim!
Crawl to the end of that crooked limb.
Carefully pick the fairest and best;
Now for a shake, and down come the rest.
Thump! *Plump*! Down they come raining!
Shake away! Shake till not one is remaining.
Hopping off here, and popping off there,
Apples and apples are everywhere.
Golden russets, with sunburnt cheek,
Fat, ruddy Baldwins, jolly and sleek;
Pippins, not much when they meet your eyes,
But wait till you see them in tarts and pies!
Where are the Pumpkin Sweets? Oh, here!
Where are the Northern Spies! Oh, there!
And there are the Nodheads, and here the Snows,
And yonder the Porder, best apple that grows.
Beautiful Bellefleurs, yellow as gold,
Think not we're leaving you out in the cold;
And dear fat Greenings, so prime to bake,
I'll eat of you now, for true love's sake.
Oh, bright is the autumn sun o'erhead,
And bright are the piles of gold and red!
And rosy and bright as the apples themselves
Are Jim, Tom and Harry, as merry as elves.

The recipes on the following pages are from my collection of heirloom apple recipes that my mother, her mother and her two sisters used in their everyday cooking. ❖

Fried Apples

⅓ cup butter
6 cups sliced, tart cooking apples
¼ cup brown sugar
⅛ teaspoon salt
1 teaspoon cinnamon
⅛ teaspoon nutmeg

Melt butter in large skillet. Add apples, brown sugar and salt. Cook, uncovered, over low heat for 15 minutes or until the apples are tender. Sprinkle with spices. Serve warm.

A cast-iron skillet filled with delicious fried apples. Photograph by Janice Tate.

Apple Corn Bread

3 cooking apples, peeled, cored
   and sliced
1 teaspoon lemon juice
½ cup cornmeal
1 cup all-purpose flour
2½ teaspoons baking powder
⅓ teaspoon salt
¼ teaspoon baking soda
⅓ cup butter, melted
¼ cup sugar
1 egg
¼ cup molasses or honey
¾ cup milk

Topping
¼ cup sugar
1 teaspoon ground cinnamon

Preheat oven to 375 degrees. Grease an 8-inch square baking pan.

Sprinkle sliced apples with the lemon juice; set aside. Mix sugar and cinnamon for topping in a small bowl; set aside.

In a large bowl, mix the remaining ingredients in the order given and pour into the baking pan. Arrange apple slices on the batter and sprinkle with topping. Bake for 20 to 25 minutes, or until apples are tender. Cut into squares and serve with cream or Vanilla Sauce (recipe follows).

Vanilla Sauce

1 cup sugar
2 tablespoons flour
Cream
2 tablespoons butter
1 cup boiling water
1 teaspoon vanilla
¼ teaspoon nutmeg

In a saucepan, mix sugar and flour. Add enough cream to make a paste. Add butter; stir in boiling water. Cook for 5 minutes over medium heat. Remove from heat; stir in vanilla and nutmeg.

Apple Brown Betty

2 cups bread crumbs
½ cup butter, melted
3 cups peeled, chopped cooking apples
½ cup brown sugar
¾ teaspoon cinnamon
½ teaspoon nutmeg
1½ tablespoons lemon juice
½ cup water

Preheat oven to 350 degrees. Grease a 1½-quart baking dish.

In a medium bowl, toss bread crumbs and melted butter; set aside. In a small bowl, mix brown sugar and spices.

Sprinkle one-third of the crumbs evenly in baking dish. Cover with half the apples. Sprinkle with half the brown sugar/spice mixture. Repeat with half of the remaining crumbs and remaining apples. Mix lemon juice and water; pour over apples. Sprinkle with remaining brown sugar and spices. Top with remaining bread crumbs.

Cover and bake for 30 minutes. Uncover and bake 20 to 30 minutes longer, or until the apples are tender. Serve warm with cream or whipped cream dusted with nutmeg.

Apple Dumplings

Egg Piecrust (recipe follows)
    or other pastry for 2-crust pie

Egg Piecrust

3 cups flour
1 teaspoon salt
¾ teaspoon baking powder
1 cup lard or 1⅓ cups solid vegetable
    shortening
1 egg, beaten
⅓ cup cold water
1 tablespoon cider vinegar

Sift flour, salt and baking powder together into a large bowl. Using pastry blender, cut in half of the shortening until mixture resembles coarse cornmeal. Cut in the remaining half until pieces are the size of small peas.

Combine egg, water and vinegar. Sprinkle over the flour mixture 1 tablespoon at a time, tossing lightly with a fork until flour is moistened.

Gently form dough into two balls. Roll dough ⅛ inch thick on a lightly floured surface, rolling from the center to the edge with light strokes.

Apples

6 whole medium apples,
    peeled and cored
⅔ cup brown sugar
1 teaspoon cinnamon
2 tablespoons butter

Syrup

1 cup sugar
2 cups water
½ teaspoon cinnamon
⅛ teaspoon nutmeg
2 tablespoons butter
½ teaspoon vanilla

Preheat oven to 425 degrees. Oil a 12 x 9 x 2-inch baking pan.

Prepare Egg Piecrust (recipe follows). Roll pastry ⅛ inch thick; cut into six 7-inch squares. Place each whole apple on dough square.

Mix brown sugar and cinnamon in a small bowl. Fill apples with mixture. Top each with 1 teaspoon butter. Draw up opposite points of pastry to overlap apples. Moisten slightly with water and crimp to seal. Place dumplings in baking pan; set aside.

For syrup, mix sugar, water, cinnamon, nutmeg, butter and vanilla in a saucepan. Bring to a boil; boil for 2 minutes.

Pour hot syrup over dumplings. Bake for 10 minutes. Reduce temperature to 375 degrees and bake for 30 minutes longer, or until apples are tender. Serve warm with nutmeg-flavored cream.

Candied Apples

2 cups water
1 cup sugar
⅓ cup red cinnamon candies
6 large cooking apples, cored,
    peeled and quartered

Combine water, sugar and cinnamon candies in large saucepan. Cook over medium-high heat until candies are melted. Lower heat and cook for 10 minutes more.

Add apples to the syrup. Cook over low heat until syrup has cooked down and apples are tender but not mushy. Serve warm or cold.

Making Apple Butter

By Winnie Schuetz

Making homemade apple butter has almost become a lost art, except for some organizations whose members still know how to make it and sell the product as a fund-raiser.

I recently attended a church fest that featured a meal reminiscent of the old-time German meals served in southern Illinois. The menu consisted of bratwurst, mashed potatoes and good white gravy, sauerkraut, corn, green beans and applesauce, along with dessert and a drink. They served apple butter and bread and butter, family-style. I could tell that the apple butter was homemade.

My mother-in-law made apple butter from the time she could help stir, when she was 8 or 9 years old. Born in 1895, she passed on in 1978. It took a lot of work to produce that delicious spread. She had people from miles around who put in their orders so as not to miss out.

In 1971 I decided to help stir, just for the experience. The day before, I went to her house and helped peel the apples. That was an experience in itself. Mom's two friends came to help stir, too. They always worked together at butchering time and whenever something else came up.

We really had a jolly time that day, and we enjoyed Mom's chicken-salad sandwiches and lemonade when we took turns eating.

The next day, when the apples were well cooked down, Mom added the sugar and her secret ingredient: Red Hots candy. She also added cinnamon sticks when the texture of the apples was just right. She knew when.

Mom told me that from the time she was married in 1914, she never missed a year making apple butter. She even managed to get enough sugar during World War II. She started saving sugar right after the Christmas baking. I suppose the family had to make do with sorghum and honey. But they all enjoyed the apple butter, and it was on the table for every meal.

Below: I am helping make apple butter near my mother-in-law's 150-year-old house. Note the smokehouse behind me. My mother-in-law, Emelie Schuetz, stands to the right. Ted Heddeman is sitting on the bench; his job was to keep the fire going. Ted's wife, Ella, is sitting on the lawn chair, waiting for her turn to stir.

Even when I came into the family, in 1952, the apple butter was still eaten at meals and for snacks, or "lunches," as they called them.

In the early years of our marriage we lived in northern Illinois and visited the local homecoming sponsored by my husband's hometown, Venedy, Ill. No matter what, when we returned home, Mom always sent a half-gallon of her delicious apple butter home with us. Our family made short work of it. Once it was gone, we resigned ourselves to waiting until August rolled around again, when we could visit Mom and get another supply of that wonderful apple butter.

Sometime during the late 1950s, the Homemakers Extension gave a lesson on making slow-cooker apple butter and cooking it on the stove. I tried both, but it never, *ever* came anywhere near Mom Schuetz's delectable spread.

As I hearken back to all the hard work that was done during the Good Old Days, I often wonder if they weren't a lot better off than we are in this day and age. ❖

Delicious Doughnuts

3 tablespoons corn oil
1½ cups sugar
2 eggs
¾ teaspoon salt
1 teaspoon nutmeg
½ teaspoon cinnamon
½ cup cornstarch
4 cups flour
4 teaspoons baking powder
1 cup milk
Oil for deep frying

Beat eggs. Add 3 tablespoons corn oil, sugar, salt and spices; stir till well mixed. In a separate bowl, sift together flour, cornstarch and baking powder.

Add milk to oil/sugar mixture. Beat in flour mixture. Turn dough out onto lightly floured board. Roll ⅓ inch thick.

Cut with a doughnut cutter.

Heat oil for deep frying to 350 degrees, or until a bit of bread will brown in 1 minute. Fry doughnuts a few at a time in hot oil for 4 minutes, turning them as soon as they rise to the surface and occasionally thereafter. Drain hot doughnuts on paper towels. If desired, dust doughnuts with confectioner's sugar mixed with a little cinnamon. To freshen, warm in a hot oven for 3 to 4 minutes.

1952 Crisco ad, House of White Birches nostalgia archives

Aunt Jemima's Pancakes

By Jen Kost

Recently I was watching a television commercial for Aunt Jemima's wonderful pancakes. It reminded me that ever since childhood, I have eaten that brand of pancakes—and that has been some time. Later, while leafing through some old magazines dating to the early 1930s, I ran across Aunt Jemima's face smiling out from her ads.

Do you know who the real "Aunt Jemima" was? She was Nancy Green, and she became famous as the "advertising world's first living trademark." Did you know that Aunt Jemima pancakes were the first "ready-mixed convenience food" for us "harried homemakers"?

Nancy Green's delightful personality helped this product become a great success. Her smiling face was to be seen on store shelves all over the country. For 30 years, Nancy Green appeared in person as "Aunt Jemima" at fairs and in grocery stores the world over. One of the 1934 ads read: "Today—her secret is yours for old-time Southern pancakes."

Nancy Green became "the world's first living trademark."

Part of her legend was that her famous pancakes were always served on Colonel Higbee's plantation, and that only she knew the recipe for making them.

In reality, that recipe was thought up by Chris L. Rutt, a newspaperman, and Charles Underwood. In 1889, these two put their money together to purchase the Pearl Milling Co. of St. Joseph, Mo. Then these two enterprising men came up with the idea of developing and packaging a pancake flour, all ready-mixed and self-rising. The nation's universal love of pancakes was a sure-fire answer to the old maxim "Find a need and fill it."

Rutt came up with the name for the product after attending a minstrel show one night, where he saw a delightful black-faced performer singing a catchy tune about "Aunt Jemima." She wore an apron and a bandana tied about her head.

But, as is often the case in the competitive world of business, the imaginative duo who came up with the original ideas were low on funds. They eventually lost out because they could not adequately finance the product's development. In 1890, Rutt and Underwood lost their mix to R.T. Davis' Milling Co. The mix then became the property of this larger St. Joseph, Mo., company.

Facing page: 1962 Aunt Jemima Pancake ad, House of White Birches nostalgia archives

Hooray! It's Aunt Jemima Day

Hooray! "Order-up" Pancakes

"I want blueberries!" "Bacon for me." "May I have banana slices?" Now everybody can have his own favorite! Just shake up a batch of Aunt Jemima batter and pour. While the first side is cooking, sprinkle on blueberries, crumbled cooked bacon or maybe chopped pecans. Raisins or chocolate chips, too. Or . . . place slices of franks or bananas on griddle and pour batter over them; bake to a golden brown on each side. Good fun, and the best eating ever—Aunt Jemima "Order-up" Pancakes. Try 'em today!

Focusing on the "Aunt Jemima" name, Davis searched for an African-American woman to employ as a living trademark for the product. That's where Nancy Green literally came into the picture.

Nancy Green, a former slave who had been born in Montgomery County, Ky., was by then 59 and living in Chicago, where she worked in a judge's home. Attractive and possessing a delightful personality, she was a wonderful storyteller. She was not at all bothered by the crowds when she ably demonstrated the new pancake mix at the 1893 Chicago World's Fair, cooking pancakes on a griddle in front of the enormous flour barrel Davis exhibited.

Her ability to laugh, joke, and tell tall tales about the South to the crowd made her a favorite with fair-goers—and they loved her fluffy, light, mouthwatering pancakes.

That showing at the fair resulted in 50,000 orders for Aunt Jemima pancake mix. As Aunt Jemima, Nancy Green was awarded a medal and certificate for showmanship by the fair officials who proclaimed her the "Pancake Queen."

For some time thereafter, Davis' company did well. Nancy signed a lifetime contract with Davis, and went on promotional tours throughout the country as Aunt Jemima. Her face became well-known to American families as she smiled out at them from huge billboards and pancake-mix packages.

Later on, due to financial difficulties, the company ownership changed again. But Nancy remained "Aunt Jemima" until, on Sept. 24, 1923, she was killed by a car on Chicago's South Side. ❖

Banana-Wheat Pancakes

¾ cup whole-wheat flour
¼ cup flour
⅓ cup whole-bran cereal
2 teaspoons baking powder
Dash of salt
1¼ cups milk
2 tablespoons oil
¾ cup finely chopped banana
   (1 medium)

In mixing bowl, stir together flours, cereal, baking powder and salt. Add milk and oil. Stir to combine. Stir in banana. Using a scant ¼ cup batter for each, cook pancakes on hot, lightly greased griddle, turning once. Makes 10 to 12.
                              —*Edith Wright Holmes*

Bohemian Pancakes
These were made by my grandmother and her mother to feed their large family of nine children. My mother made these about once a week, and my sons and I enjoyed them every time.

1¼ cups flour
1 tablespoon sugar,
      plus extra for topping
½ teaspoon salt
2 eggs, well beaten
1 cup lukewarm milk
1 cake yeast, dissolved
      in a little lukewarm milk
Cinnamon

Sift flour, 1 tablespoon sugar and salt into bowl. Add beaten eggs and lukewarm milk; mix well. Add the dissolved yeast. Beat thoroughly and set in a warm place to rise until light.

Carefully lift the batter by spoonfuls from top of mixture so as not to disturb the remainder. Spread batter on well-greased griddle using back of spoon. Let bake slowly.

Serve warm with cinnamon and sugar sprinkled on top. Delicious!
                              —*Mrs. Mildred M. Eaton*

Grandma's Gritwurst

By Lila M. Konow

*M*aking sausage and putting up meat was a great part of our living when I was young. Ma made homemade sausage and canned the beef in the old-fashioned green jars in the big wash boiler on top of the old cookstove. Then she would fry down the pork chops and put them in a big stone jar with lard over them. We would eat them during the winter.

The meat was much better in those days. The roast would cook—and without shrinking, as it does today. We could make brown gravy out of the rich drippings; now there is water in the roasting pan. In those days the cattle and hogs were fed on grain, and not all of the fast-weight-gain feed of today.

This is the recipe for the *gritwurst* my grandma used to make. It has been a family treat for years. I still make it. ❖

Grandma's Gritwurst

3 pounds lean pork
1 pound pork liver
Water to cover
6 cups old-fashioned oatmeal
Salt, pepper, sage and allspice

Boil pork and liver in water to cover until tender. Drain broth from the meat; cool and refrigerate both broth and meat until very cold, or overnight. Skim the fat from the broth and grind the meat.

Heat the broth to boiling, then add the oatmeal and cook slowly. Add ground meat and spices to taste, blending well. Turn out into flat pans to cool. When cold, slice and fry in a pan with a little fat until golden brown. Makes about 8 pounds.

Pepper Hash

1 dozen red peppers
1 dozen green peppers
1 dozen medium onions
3 cups vinegar
2 cups sugar
3 tablespoons salt

Wash peppers and onions. Peel onions; remove seeds from peppers. Run peppers and onions through grinder, or chop fine. Pour boiling water over peppers and onions. Let stand for 5 minutes; drain.

Combine peppers and onions in kettle with vinegar, sugar and salt. Bring to boil and boil, stirring frequently, for 10 minutes. Put in cans and seal. Makes 13 pints.

—*Mrs. Walde H. Griggs*

Advent Gravy

During World War I, we made this gravy, called Advent Gravy, as learned from Adventists.

6 tablespoons sour cream
Water or milk (see Note)
Flour for thickening

Put sour cream in heavy frying pan. Cook, stirring with spatula so as not to burn, until it is like oil with specks of meat in it.

Stir in water or milk; add flour and cook, stirring, until thickened and bubbly.

Note: I like to use water in which potatoes were boiled.

—*Mrs. Harry Babcock*

Home-Baked Memories

Chapter Two

Grandma Tate always baked me a peach cobbler for my birthday. It was a yearly ritual that I revered. Grandma and Grandpa Tate had 13 children; 11 survived to adulthood and had a passel of youngsters themselves.

When it came to birthdays, Grandma always provided a special present. Each grandchild was allowed to pick his or her favorite dessert and Grandma baked it. Grandma's old-fashioned peach cobbler was my favorite, hands down. So that became my home-baked birthday treat every October.

I married a great pie-maker. My waistline will attest to that. Janice can whip up a pie from just about anything. If "the way to a man's heart is through his stomach," it's no wonder I love her so!

But as great a pie-maker as Janice is, she never thought of herself as much of a cobbler-maker.

One late fall day I carried in an armload of wood to find two steaming apple pies on the table. Something about the crisp fall day and the pies fresh from the oven jogged a memory.

"Honey, would you make me a peach cobbler?" I pleaded. I knew it wouldn't be her first choice, so I quickly added: "I *know* you can bake one as good as Grandma used to make!"

My dear wife sighed, blew the dust off her cobbler recipe and, when it was pie-baking time again, I had my peach cobbler.

As I cut into the cobbler after supper, the sweet cinnamon-and-peach scent wafted upward and suddenly I was a youngster again, sitting at Grandma's kitchen table and enjoying my yearly special treat.

It was a delicious moment, even if Janice didn't think her cobbler passed muster. I don't think she realized that what I was tasting were the home-baked memories of yesteryear.

—*Ken Tate*

> *If "the way to a man's heart is through his stomach," it's no wonder I love her so!*

Old-Fashioned Peach Cobbler

        Pastry for 2-crust, 9-inch pie
        10 cups sliced, peeled peaches
        3 tablespoons butter or margarine
        1 cup sugar
        ½ cup cornstarch
        ½ teaspoon cinnamon
        ⅛ teaspoon salt

About 2 hours ahead or early in day

Preheat oven to 425 degrees. On large floured surface with floured rolling pin, roll out three-fourths of the pastry into 18 x 12-inch rectangle; use to line 12 x 8 inch baking dish. Spoon peaches into dish; dot with butter or margarine. In small bowl, stir sugar with cornstarch, cinnamon and salt; sprinkle over peaches.

Roll remaining pastry into 10 x 6-inch rectangle. With pastry cutter, cut dough lengthwise into six 1-inch strips; place crosswise over peaches. Fold edges of bottom crust up over strip ends, pinching to seal.

Bake 50 minutes or until filling is bubbly and crust is golden. Let stand 15 minutes, then serve warm. Add vanilla ice cream for a special touch. Can also be cooled completely, makes 10 servings.

Baking Bread With Mom

By Ralph W. Logay

After my mom passed away, I had the sad job of cleaning out her house. In the kitchen I came across a small metal box filled with yellowing recipe cards. I glanced through the first few and saw that they were blank. I grabbed the whole handful and pitched them into the garbage can. One of the index cards fell out onto the floor. I almost shoved it back into the trash, but then I noticed some writing on it.

The handwritten title was "Home-Made-Bread." I stared at my mom's writing and felt her close to me for a moment. An image of Mom pushing up pointy glasses with the back of her hand drifted into my mind. Because of an injury to her hand when she was a teenager, her little finger always jutted out in a dainty pose, reminiscent of the way the Queen of England must have held her teacup.

I looked over the worn card and wondered if it was the same bread recipe that my mother always made for the holidays. I stuffed the card in my pants pocket and went on cleaning her kitchen. When I got home, I threw my dirty jeans in the corner of the garage and forgot about them.

A year later, while cleaning out my garage, I came across that soiled pair of jeans. I tossed them into the garbage and saw that piece of paper sticking out of the back pocket. Curious, I plucked it out and realized that it was the bread recipe. As a child, I used to help my mom bake the bread. She'd ask, "Honey, could you get me a wooden spoon from the drawer?" I'd grab the spoon from the drawer and give it to her.

I was assigned the duty of shutting off the pan of scalded milk just as it started to foam. She would say, "Don't let the milk boil over."

I never took my eyes off the pan. "Don't worry, Ma," I said.

Why milk must be scalded, I never knew. It was just how my grandmother did it. Yes, the recipe card called for scalded milk.

I decided then that I must bake a loaf of that bread. I gave up cleaning the garage—I didn't want to do it anyway—and went to the grocery store instead, clutching the dog-eared recipe card in my hand.

Many years before, I had shopped with Mom. She let me push the cart and retrieve various items from the store shelves. Maybe that's why, even today, I don't mind grocery shopping.

Those decades ago, Mom made shopping fun. She would assign me an item to find and I would dash through the store in search of it. When I brought back the right item, she would smile as a reward and place the item into our cart. She always made the mundane enjoyable.

As I checked out, I recalled Mom laughing at my struggle to carry the paper bags out to the car. I rushed home with this day's plastic bag of groceries.

As I read through the recipe card's instructions, memories of Mom, family gatherings and the heady smells of home cooking filled my mind. I thought, *I can do this.*

Then I made another discovery. In my cupboard I had an old glass mixing bowl taken from my mom's kitchen. It was the same bowl that had held the precious dough so many years before. This would be the bowl in which I would mix this day's dough.

Soon flour was all over the kitchen. The sink was filled with utensils, and eureka! the dough was mixed!

As I scraped my finger inside the bowl, I could almost hear my mom say, "Don't eat

---

Memories of my mother's love for me seemed to be carried on the fragrance of the baked bread.

---

too much of that raw dough; it'll blow up your stomach." Of course, it never did.

Then it was time to wait patiently for the bread to rise. I put on an old Perry Como tape that I had taken from Mom's house. I dug out some old pictures of her and Dad at family gatherings from long ago. I placed the pan in the oven and was immediately transported back to my childhood. The memories I retrieved were as real as anything in the present. Mom lived on.

Voilà!

The timer went off and the bread was done. Then for the eating. The golden loaf cooled while I put away the old photos and played more modern music. The bouquet of the baked bread was intoxicating. I could have been in my mom's kitchen, decades ago. The aroma was exactly the same.

Memories of my mother's love for me and mine for her seemed to be carried on the fragrance of the baked bread. Carefully I sliced off the heel and cut a regular slice.

As I always did in my youth, I slathered the slice with real butter and sprinkled granulated

1931 Magic Yeast ad, House of White Birches nostalgia archives

Mom's Homemade Bread

1½ packages dry yeast
¼ cup warm water (110 degrees)

1⅓ cups milk   ½ cup sugar
2 teaspoons salt   5 eggs, lightly beaten
3 tablespoons butter   5 cups flour
Additional softened butter

Grease 1 large or 2 smaller loaf pans.

Mix dry yeast with warm water. Scald milk, then add sugar, salt, eggs and 3 tablespoons butter. Cool 5 minutes in cool water bath. Add yeast and water to cooled milk mixture. Mix in flour, adding it gradually, until dough is fairly stiff. Knead with hands in bowl until well blended.

Rub top of dough with softened butter. Cover with moist towel and let rise in warm place until about double in bulk. Punch down gently, then form into loaf and place in greased baking pan. Rub top again with butter and let rise again.

Preheat oven to 375 degrees. Bake bread for 30 to 40 minutes, or until loaf sounds hollow when tapped. Let cool. Slice and serve with butter and sugar. Makes 1 large loaf or 2 smaller loaves.

sugar all over it. A sip of ice-cold milk accompanied the first bite.

I felt as if Mom had prepared the bread for me—and in a way, she did. For just a joyful moment, I sensed that she was there with me.

In my heart, she was. Here is the original recipe for homemade bread.

As my grandmother made it, my mom watched her and wrote down the ingredients. Enjoy! ❖

Christmas Cranberries

By Isabel Miller

Mr. Clement, would you care for some cranberry sarce?"—Kate Douglas Wiggins, *The Birds' Christmas Carol*. 1916.

There they were—cranberries for Christmas. How clean and shiny they looked in their sparkling cellophane packages. I could almost imagine that Mother Nature had sat up all night waxing and polishing them for their big day.

If it hadn't been for an early teaching experience, I don't suppose cranberries would have meant more to me than what they are in the store—bright, shiny berries to be taken home to make ruby-red sauce for Christmas.

One autumn, a school in the North was without a teacher, and I found myself teaching in the land of pine and muskeg, living in a log cabin on the banks of the river. "There are cranberries down in the muskeg," they told me. "Just walk out through the pasture and down the trail."

So, every night after supper, I walked down the path, through the cool quiet of the evening, to where the cranberries were. I found them hiding modestly under the sparse leaves in the muskeg. Picking them was not very easy. The berries were few and far between. I think the patch had been well-picked over, but there is a satisfaction in finding berries where at first glance there was none.

I had music while I worked, too, a wonderful nocturnal symphony: cowbell tinkling in the distance; a crow bossily cawing his last-minute instructions to a sleepy world;

and the muted sounds from the farm—the clatter of milk pails and the occasional bark of the dog.

When it was too dark to pick any longer, I made my way back to the house with my pail of berries. Little by little my store grew.

The berries were much smaller than the kind I had bought in stores, but they tasted the same. When frost and a light snowfall put an end to my picking, I brought my berries back home and we had real, hand-picked cranberry sauce for Christmas that year.

According to my horticulture book, cranberries are cousins of blueberries and are particular about where they grow. Like blueberries, they require an acid soil.

(Just to set us straight, the record goes on to say that the so-called "high-bush cranberry" is not a cranberry at all, but a Pembina berry, which makes good jelly but is not good for "sarce" because its seeds are too big.)

Cranberries—the big, red ones—come mostly from the New England states. The United States crop of berries is well over a million barrels, which would make a lot more sauce than I would care to cook up all by myself. ❖

Cranberry-Orange Bread

2 cups flour
1 cup sugar
1½ teaspoons baking powder
½ teaspoon baking soda
½ teaspoon salt
2 tablespoons shortening
Grated rind and juice of 1 orange plus water to make ¾ cup
1 egg, beaten
1 cup raw cranberries, cut in halves

Heat oven to 350 degrees. Grease a 9½ x 5½ x 3½-inch loaf pan. Blend flour, sugar, baking powder, baking soda and salt. Mix in shortening, orange rind with juice and water, and beaten egg. Fold in cranberries. Pour batter into pan. Bake for 1 hour. Cool thoroughly before slicing with a thin, sharp knife.

Dough for the Ages

By Alice Jacksha

On Saturdays mornings my husband, Leo, fixes his specialty, sourdough pancakes and sausages. When I hear the smoke alarm go off, I know it's time to eat. Leo says, "These are the best pancakes you ever flung a lip over," and I do believe he is right. It's no wonder that sourdough has been handed down through the ages.

Sourdough is fermented dough saved from one baking to another to use in place of fresh yeast, which was at a premium at various times throughout history. It is made from flour and dry yeast, or from wild yeast started from soured raw milk.

Some purists say milk shouldn't be added to the starter. We put milk in ours, but we use some starter once a week to keep it fresh. It can also be refrigerated or frozen.

Yukon prospectors used to freeze it and cut off a chunk when they needed it. Hobos riding the rails carried a wad of sourdough in their pockets to use later with whatever else they could find to eat. (My brother-in-law used to do that.) Wild yeast was used to make beer thousands of years before the birth of Christ. Later, people discovered that it could be used to make their bread rise, and sourdough came into being. In ancient times, bread made from sourdough was used for wages and even for making plates and eating utensils.

> *During pioneer days, sourdough was used for glue, salves and poultices.*

During pioneer days, sourdough was used for glue, salves and poultices, besides being used to make beer, bread, biscuits and flapjacks (American pancakes). It also was used for polishing metals and for chinking log cabins.

With the influx of European immigrants came sourdough pots for making beer and bread. Flour mills and breweries were soon established in the settlements.

When wagons moved westward, so did the sourdough pots. Gold fever took people to California and the Yukon where sourdough, beans and fresh meat were the main foods. The word *sourdough* soon became synonymous with *prospector.*

Mom's ancestors came from Germany (the Wegeners) about 1881 and from Norway (the Gjernesses) in 1870. Dad's ancestors came from England (the Everetts) about 1620 and from Germany (the Stellrechts) in the 1880s. They probably brought sourdough pots with them, as most of the immigrants did in those days.

The eldest Everett son remained in England on the family estate. His brothers, Richard, David and John, came to America and settled in Massachusetts and Maine. From there they branched out to other

states. Eight generations down the line, Richard Everett's descendant, Charles Edwin Everett, came to Minnesota, bringing his wife and five children with him. The eldest was my grandfather, William Henry.

William was a carpenter and built houses in many towns on the Iron Range. Somewhere along the way he met a lovely little lady named Marie Rosina Stellrecht. They fell in love and got married.

William built a log cabin along a trout stream in the North Woods, just three miles from where I now live. It was wilderness then, where mountain lions and timber wolves roamed. Marie was so frightened of the mountain lions that she pulled the ladder up into the sleeping loft at night, not realizing that they could have climbed up the pole next to the ladder.

As time went by, they had five children: Mildred, Vivian, Everyll, Clarence and James. Believe it or not, Vivian was a boy, not a girl— he was my dad!

There were many logging railroads throughout northern Minnesota at that time. Of course, sourdough was used in the logging camps for making bread and flapjacks. My dad worked in a logging camp when he was young, as did my husband when he was 14.

A logging railroad went right through the land where my parents later built a house and raised us four children. Grandpa Everett had given that piece of land to Dad. The adjoining land was given to Dad's sister, Everyll.

My brother Jim and I often crossed the rapids to visit Grandpa Everett. He was living alone then as Grandma had passed away and all his children were grown and gone. He was always so glad to see us and to show us how to make potato soup, rice pudding and sourdough pancakes. There always was a crock of sourdough on the back of his wood stove. Grandpa passed away during World War II.

In 1951, I married an iron-ore miner named Leo Jacksha. He was pretty handy at flipping pancakes in a little, tin frying pan. It looked easy so I decided to try it, too. I poured in some batter, let it cook awhile, loosened the pancake a little with a spatula, then flipped it confidently into the air. It came down half in the pan and half on the stove. Maybe it wasn't as easy as I thought.

Here we are, four children, 55 years and thousands of pancakes later, living out in the country. We still make pancakes, and always have a jar of sourdough sitting on the cupboard. I just don't know how we would get along without sourdough. It has been around for thousands of years and will probably be around long after I'm gone. It might even go to the moon or to other planets with the astronauts, on to a new frontier and a new era!

Sourdough forever!

Here are some of our favorite recipes. I hope you will enjoy them. ❖

Sourdough Starter

1½ teaspoons dry yeast
2½ cups warm water
2 cups flour
2 tablespoons sugar

Mix all ingredients. Let stand overnight or longer in a warm place. Put it in a large bowl at first because it runs over. After that, put it in a glass jar and cover it tightly.

To Replenish Starter

Add 1½ cups lukewarm water, 1½ cups flour and 1½ teaspoons sugar; stir and let set overnight. If it spoils, save about 4 tablespoons from bottom, and add water, flour and sugar to start it over again.

Sourdough Bread

5 to 6 cups flour, divided
3 tablespoons sugar
1 tablespoon salt
1 tablespoon (1 package) dry yeast
1 cup milk
3 tablespoons oil
1½ cups sourdough starter

Combine 2 cups flour, sugar, salt and yeast in a large bowl. Combine milk and oil in a pan and heat until warm, not hot. Add to dry ingredients and beat well with mixer. Add sourdough starter and 1 cup flour to make a thick batter. Beat well.

Add enough flour to make stiff dough. Knead until smooth and elastic.

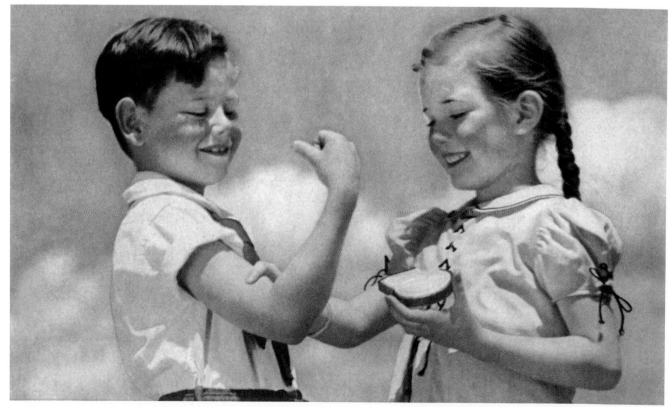

Place in greased bowl, turning to grease top. Cover; let rise in a warm place until doubled. Punch dough in half, shape, and place in greased loaf pans. Let rise and bake for 45 to 55 minutes at 350 degrees.

Makes 2 loaves.

Sourdough Pancakes

1 cup sourdough starter
2 cups milk
2 cups flour
1 teaspoon salt
2 teaspoons baking soda
2 eggs
3 tablespoons oil
2 tablespoons sugar

Mix sourdough starter, milk, flour and salt thoroughly with a whisk. Return 1 cup of mixture to container of sourdough starter. To remaining mixture in bowl, add baking soda, eggs, vegetable oil and sugar.

Fry on a hot, lightly greased griddle. Makes thin, tasty pancakes. Unused batter can be stored in refrigerator. Serves 4 to 5.

Multigrain Sourdough Pancakes

⅔ cup flour
⅓ cup whole-wheat flour
⅓ cup rye, buckwheat or graham flour
¼ cup yellow cornmeal
2 tablespoons sugar
2 teaspoons baking powder
1 teaspoon salt
½ teaspoon baking soda
2 cups buttermilk or 1⅓ cups
    regular milk
2 large eggs
1 tablespoon light molasses
2 tablespoons oil

Mix flours, cornmeal, sugar, baking powder, salt and baking soda. In a large bowl, beat milk, eggs, molasses and oil until well blended.

Add flour mixture; stir until moistened.

Bake on hot, lightly greased griddle. Makes about 14 pancakes. Any remaining batter can be refrigerated or fried up and reheated later. My granddaughters like cold pancakes with butter and sugar on them—and so do I.

Variation for Waffles

Separate the eggs; whip the whites and fold them in last. Baked waffles can be frozen, then popped into the toaster to reheat.

Homemade Maple Syrup

4 cups sugar
½ cup brown sugar
2 to 3 tablespoons light corn syrup
2 cups water
1 teaspoon pure vanilla
1 to 2 teaspoons maple flavoring
    (I use Crescent Mapleine)

Combine all ingredients in a large pot over medium heat. Bring to a boil and boil for about 5 minutes, stirring constantly.

This makes about 2 quarts of thick, delicious syrup that tastes as good as store syrup, but has no preservatives. After it has cooled, it should be refrigerated so it won't get moldy.

Family Heirloom

By Gloria Ericson

Most families have at least one recipe that is carefully handed down from mother to daughter through the generations. In my family that recipe is for Elephant Bread. It's an oatmeal tea bread, with a cinnamony fragrance that drives us all quite wild while it bakes, and causes us to fall like ravenous wolves on the first loaf to come out of the oven.

Yes, we know—intellectually at least—that you shouldn't cut into hot bread, but the sensuous pleasure of watching refrigerator-cold butter melt into an aromatic, steaming slice of Elephant Bread is too much to resist.

When my mother was alive, I asked her several times how it got its name, but she didn't seem to know. "Maybe it was named for its color," she suggested.

"But elephants are gray, not brown," I objected.

"Well, maybe it was called that because it's heavy—like an elephant." But she really didn't know, and the origin of the name has been lost to us.

My mother, when she made the bread, always made enough for two or three loaves. But she also saved enough dough so that she could put large dollops of it on a cookie sheet. In the oven, the dollops spread out to a pancake's width and half the height of a muffin. I remember that as a small child, I thought that if the loaves were called Elephant Bread, the rounded shapes must be Elephant Feet.

Over the years I tampered with the recipe, hoping to upgrade it nutritionally: I changed the solid shortening to vegetable oil, and substituted wheat germ for some of the flour. But I was careful not to add anything that would change the taste.

1939 Nucoa Oleomargarine ad, House of White Birches nostalgia archives

When my older daughter went off to college, she took the recipe with her. I was upset to hear that to upgrade it even further she had added some soy flour and milk powder to it. But she reassured me. "Don't worry, Mom," she said. "It still tastes like Elephant Bread." I tasted some and relaxed.

But then she gave the recipe to a male college chum who was into cooking and health food, and he added all manner of things. She tried it and found that the old familiar Elephant Bread taste had finally succumbed.

Distraught, she stormed at him: "That is *not* Elephant Bread! If you make it that way, you cannot *call* it Elephant Bread!" Fortunately, he was an amicable fellow.

"OK," he said, laughing. "I'll call mine Gnu Bread."

Whew! It was a close call—one that made both my daughter and me realize that only family members understood what was allowable in tampering and what was not. After all, the recipe undoubtedly had been tampered with by family members before it got to me.

For instance, the copy my mother wrote out for me lists "Crisco" as the shortening to be used. But Crisco hasn't been around forever, and I would be willing to bet that *her* mother's copy of the recipe called for lard.

I still have the original recipe my mother gave me, written in pencil on lined copybook paper. It is very dog-eared; grease spots have made the paper almost transparent in places.

I keep saying that I must copy it over on a sturdy card, or perhaps even feed it into my home computer, so that pristine copies can be run off at will. But somehow I haven't done that. If I handle the recipe very carefully, it will last as long as I will.

I like handling the original recipe. I like

My daughter really should have her own handwritten copy.

seeing my mother's handwriting—and my own spidery notes in the margins where I have tried to anchor the old-fashioned directions to more mathematically precise terms.

The recipe is replete with such instructions as "take a half-cup of Crisco (generous)." How much is *that* exactly?

Or: "Add a half-box of raisins." But the full-pound box of raisins of my mother's day has shrunk to 15, 14, even 13½ ounces, and probably doesn't hold *that* much. And when the recipe says to "add hot water to cover the raisins," I tried to pin my mother down on exactly how much that was, and noted it on the side.

Lately I have been thinking: My older daughter has a copy of the recipe, but my younger one doesn't. Someday I will write it out for her. And I fancy her, years hence, after I am gone, propping her batter-spattered copy against her cabinet, and thinking that she really should copy it over, but not getting around to it until one day, when she realizes that her own daughter should have a handwritten copy. ❖

Elephant Bread

1 teaspoon baking soda
2¾ to 3¼ cups water, divided
2 cups old-fashioned oatmeal
½ pound raisins (approximately 1½ cups)
1½ cups brown sugar
½ cup plus 2 tablespoons oil
6 cups flour (see Note)
1 tablespoon salt
4 teaspoons baking powder
2 teaspoons cinnamon
1 teaspoon ginger
1 teaspoon nutmeg

Note: 1 cup wheat germ may be substituted for 1 cup of the flour.

The evening before: Dissolve baking soda in ¼ cup water. Pour over oatmeal, raisins, brown sugar and oil. Moisten these ingredients with hot water to cover (approximately 2½ cups), and let stand overnight.

In the morning: Preheat oven to 350 degrees. Grease 3 loaf pans. Combine the rest of the dry ingredients and add them to the moistened ingredients. You will probably have to add a little more water, as the dough must be moist and sticky. Divide among loaf pans and bake for approximately 1 hour.

One More Slice

By Janice I. Kinman

Boys are always hungry. In the early 1940s, my husband, Les, and his brothers, Richard and Charles, were no exception. Frequently one or the other stomped into the kitchen and piteously whined, "I'm hungry. Isn't dinner ready yet?"

Their stepmother, Minnie, struggled to hold the grocery bill to a minimum. The Depression was over, but money was scarce. Necessarily she supervised and regulated food portions at the table. The young trio, not exposed to finances, considered her mean and talked about her behind her back. When she denied them food they implored, "What are you trying to do? Starve us?"

As Les recalled his boyhood, I remembered our two sons in their early years. Snacks were always in demand—even a slice of bread. "Yes, one slice," I answered, and then shooed them out of the kitchen until lunch was ready.

In Les' house, low-cost meals of bread and gravy often were the main course for a family of seven. Sometimes the gravy wasn't much more than clear thickened broth containing very little flavor. Two slices of bread were rationed per child. On "gravy day," if Minnie wasn't in sight, the boys slapped a slice of white bread on their plate and ladled gravy over it. With practiced skill and speed they could slap, cover and eat a serving in record time.

While swallowing the last mouthful, they reached for another slice and slathered it with more gravy before their stepmother re-entered the kitchen. She never detected that the boys gained an extra portion, or she never let on.

Sometimes when they were outside playing cops and robbers or soldiers in combat, hunger got the best of them. At the slightest suggestion—"A slice of bread would sure taste good"—appetites were whetted.

After an informal vote, Richard, the middle brother, was dispatched into the house, because "You're the sneakiest." While the other two hid out of sight and promised, "We'll stand guard for you," he stealthily crouched, crawled and tiptoed into the kitchen.

He reached the cabinet with the big bottom drawer where bread was stored. Silently, Richard retrieved three slices of bread, eased the drawer shut and in exaggerated giant steps, exited the house as quietly as he had entered. Clearing the porch, he broke into a dead run. In a loud whisper he hissed, "Come on, I got it!"

With two accomplices hot on his heels, the brave hero headed for a small grove of trees at the edge of the yard. A safe distance from the house, they dropped breathlessly onto the grass under a huge oak tree, and divided the loot.

Les chuckled and declared, "Boy, that bread tasted good!" The three youngsters fancied themselves secret agents with mission accomplished.

It is coincidence perhaps, but 60 years later, the oldest brother sometimes lifts the lid on our bread box noiselessly and expertly slips out a slice of bread. With a boyish grin, he glances my way and explains, "Just to tide me over until mealtime." ❖

Mama Made Zupfe

By Marianne Severson

When the day dawns gray and gloomy, and the sky is overcast, I roll up my sleeves and set to work baking bread. The smell of bread baking always brings memories of happy days at my mother's side. I could barely see over the top of the table.

Every holiday, Mama made *zupfe*, a Swiss egg bread. "Zupfe" means "to braid."

It was the day before Easter. The smell of yeast greeted my nostrils as I watched Mama, fascinated. Mama dropped the cake of gray yeast into the warm water and it bubbled up.

Mixing the ingredients, she rolled the mixture into a huge ball and placed it in the mixing bowl. She covered it, then placed it someplace warm, away from cold drafts. After about an hour, we could see the dough had risen under the cloth, pushing the covering up in the center. Mama uncovered it and punched the dough down, then covered it again. After it had doubled in size once more, she worked the dough, kneading it on the floured breadboard with the heels of her palms.

When she had kneaded it enough, she divided the dough into six balls. She formed three of the balls into long strands and braided them together. "Just like I braid your hair." She formed a second loaf with the remaining dough, then covered them and left them to rise again.

Just then, my brother, Herb, burst into the kitchen after delivering his paper route. "Mmm, it smells so good. Anything to eat?" Mama obliged. It took her a while to make it, but when she took the golden brown loaves of braided zupfe out of the oven, it was all worth it.

After I married and moved away, I called Mama to ask about making zupfe. "How long do you knead the zupfe?" I might have known what her reply would be: "Just until it feels right."

I persisted. "But Mom, how do you know how long to knead the zupfe?" Her brown eyes smiled as she replied, "Well, I say the Lord's Prayer while I knead the dough."

When my daughter, Judy, asked me to bake the zupfe for her Easter dinner, I remembered Mama's words. As I kneaded the dough, I said the Lord's Prayer, then repeated it slowly for good measure. At Easter dinner the next day, the ultimate compliment rang in my ears. "Mmm, it's good as Grandma's!" ❖

Zupfe

1 (2-ounce) cake of yeast
  or 2 packages dry yeast
½ cup warm (not hot) water
1 teaspoon sugar
1 tablespoon salt

3 eggs, beaten, divided
2 cups milk
½ cup (1 stick) butter
5 to 6 cups flour

Add yeast to warm water, then add sugar. Let set until it bubbles. Scald milk; let cool. Add salt and butter to milk. Add yeast to milk mixture. Add 2 beaten eggs to milk mixture; blend.

Sift 3 cups flour into the mixture and beat well. Add enough additional flour—2 to 3 cups—to make a soft dough. Place in greased bowl; grease top of dough. Cover and let rise in a warm place free from drafts until double in bulk, about 1 hour.

Punch dough down, then knead and let rise again until doubled. Knead again and divide into six equal portions. Form each into a rope and braid three together, making two loaves. Cover and let rise.

Brush tops of braided loaves with beaten egg. Let rise until double in bulk. Bake at 375 degrees for 30 to 45 minutes, or until golden brown and done. Makes 2 loaves.

Note: Zupfe is best served warm with unsalted butter.

Gingerbread Boys

By Helen K. Mitchell

During the Depression years, back in the 1930s, money was very tight. I marvel now that we couldn't afford even a few pennies to buy valentines for our friends. But we always had gingerbread-boy cookies, one for each of our classmates. Though we had very little cash, we always had plenty to eat.

We lived on a farm, and back then, my father would take a load of grain to the mill each year and have some of it ground into flour for our year's supply. This would furnish our family with bread, cereal and other baked goods.

Besides my parents, there were eight siblings in our home, four girls and four boys. My oldest sister, Velma Keller, left school at an early age to help care for our mother, who had health problems. Velma became a master at cooking, which was a big job, as she prepared meals for our farmhands as well as our family.

It was this dear sister who made gingerbread-boy cookies and decorated them with an artist's touch. Any child was delighted to receive one of her prized cookies, carefully iced and decorated with chocolate chips, raisins and candy.

Our second-grade class' Valentine's Day party at school was almost over. Valentines had been given out, and I was worried that my "valentines" wouldn't make it. My dear sister was at home finishing up the gingerbread boys.

Finally she arrived with a big box of beautifully decorated cookies. I was so proud when I had the privilege of passing out my valentines.

After I got a family of my own, another sister, Marvel, would send a big box of undecorated gingerbread boys for my children to frost and decorate. Then I started making my own, and it became a tradition in my home to make gingerbread boys for my own family, our children's friends and the neighbors. We shared dozens of cookies for Thanksgiving, Christmas, Valentine's Day, and for fund-raising projects.

We also have shared our recipe with others. This tradition has been in our family for many years. My children love them— and so do our grandchildren! ❖

Old-Fashioned Gingerbread Cookies

- 1 cup shortening
- 1 cup sugar
- 1 egg
- 2 cups molasses
- 2 tablespoons cider vinegar
- 7 cups flour plus additional flour for rolling
- 1 tablespoon ginger
- ½ teaspoon cinnamon
- ¼ teaspoon nutmeg
- 4 teaspoons baking soda
- 1 teaspoon salt
- 1 cup boiling water

Cream together shortening and sugar. Add egg; beat well. Add molasses and vinegar. Sift together 7 cups flour, ginger, cinnamon, nutmeg, baking soda and salt. Add to creamed mixture. Add hot water to mixture in three equal batches, mixing well after each addition. Refrigerate mixture just until it is stiff enough to roll.

Preheat oven to 350 degrees. On floured surface, roll dough out ¼ inch thick; cut with gingerbread boy cookie cutter. Bake 8 minutes or until brown.

Baking Cookies

By Helen Colwell Oakley

Nothing seems to lend an air of magic to a home quite like the delicious scent of baking cookies. I'm happy to say that baking cookies was just as exciting and enchanting in my early days on the farm in New York state during the Great Depression as it is today. When I arrived home after walking a mile or two from the little one-room school, chilled and tired, it was heavenly to inhale the delicious aroma of homemade cookies as I neared the door of our country kitchen. A glass of milk and several of Mom's cartwheel cookies did wonders to revive my sisters, brothers and me.

There were no chocolate chip cookies at this time, but Mom's sugar, chocolate and molasses cookies were the best. Mom's cookies would cost a fortune to purchase today, but in those long-ago days, she could bake a batch for pennies. Her cookies had a delicate flavor that is impossible to duplicate—perhaps because she used pork lard and fresh brown eggs from our very own chickens.

Mom and the ladies of yesterday would be shocked to see the prices of cookies in today's bakeries and supermarkets. Mom used to buy several dozen at a penny apiece. And when she baked cookies, her recipe would fill a huge canister with dozens of cartwheel cookies.

My mom usually stuck to the basics—sugar, chocolate and molasses cookies—but when she had time, she made cookies filled with jelly or apples that were out of this world. What a treat it was to find several of Mom's homemade cookies in our lunch pail at school!

As youngsters, we could always tell Mom's cookies from those she bought at the bakery in town. Mom's were always browned on the edges, which made them all the more tasty to us.

At holiday time, the moms in our neighborhood would go creative, turning out the most adorable cookies imaginable, with pink hearts and tarts for St. Valentine's Day, and colorful, decorated Easter and Christmas cookies. The ladies back then made parties more festive with decorative cookies; even plain, everyday get-togethers were somehow special when fresh-baked cookies were popped out of the oven.

The pantries of yesterday were magical with containers filled with home-baked cookies. Appetites improved dramatically on days when Mom worked at her stove, turning out trays of deliciously scented cookies. In long-ago times, the gift of home-baked cookies was treasured, especially by the ill. Down through the years we treasure them still.

Pleasures from our heritage seem to come and go, but baking cookies remains an enchanting, home-style ritual that has brought pleasure from earlier times to our present day. It does my heart good to see that the youngsters of today go for cookies just as we once did. ❖

Old-Fashioned Sugar Cookies
These cookies are from my friend Mary McKinney. Her cookies were truly delicious, and reminiscent of my mom's famous cartwheel cookies.

> 2 cups sugar
> 1 cup shortening
> 3 eggs
> 1 cup milk
> 1 teaspoon baking soda
> Sprinkle of salt
> Vanilla
> 2½–3 cups flour
> Flour for rolling

Preheat oven to 350 degrees. Combine all ingredients. Roll and cut. Bake for 8 minutes, or until very light brown.

—*Mary McKinney*

Sour Cream Cookies
This recipe from my good friend is her grandma's delicious cookie recipe.

> 1 cup sour cream
> ½ cup butter
> 2 cups sugar
> 2 eggs
> 1 teaspoon baking soda
> 2 teaspoons baking powder
> Pinch of salt
> ⅓ teaspoon ground nutmeg
> Approximately 4 cups flour

Preheat oven to 375 degrees. Blend all ingredients. Roll and cut with cookie cutter or drop from a spoon. Bake until brown.

—*"Grandma Bailey*

Spicy Molasses Cookies
These are thick and chewy and filled with old-fashioned goodness.

> ¾ cup softened shortening
> 1 cup brown sugar
> 1 egg
> ¼ cup molasses
> 2¼ cups flour
> 2 teaspoons baking soda
> ½ teaspoon ground cloves
> 1 teaspoon ground cinnamon
> 1 teaspoon ground ginger
> ¼ teaspoon salt
> Sugar for sprinkling
> Water for sprinkling

Blend together shortening, brown sugar, egg and molasses. Sift dry ingredients into shortening mixture and blend thoroughly. Chill dough.

Preheat oven to 375 degrees. Roll out dough; cut into 2½-inch circles. Sprinkle tops with sugar, then a few drops of water for crackled tops. Bake for 10 to 12 minutes.

—*Helen Colwell Oakley*

Ultimate Sugar Cookies
These are large, old-fashioned cartwheel cookies like Mom used to bake.

> 1¾ cups sugar
> 1 cup butter, lard or shortening
> 2 eggs
> ¼ cup syrup
> 1 teaspoon vanilla
> 3 cups flour
> ¾ teaspoon baking powder
> ½ teaspoon baking soda

Preheat oven to 375 degrees. Cream together sugar, butter and eggs; add syrup and vanilla. Sift together flour, baking powder and baking soda; blend into creamed mixture. Bake for 8 to 10 minutes.

—*Helen Colwell Oakley*

The Secret Ingredient

By Paul Eckhardt

Aunt Hannah was big and jolly while her husband, George, was tall, thin and quiet. They could have posed for Grant Wood's *American Gothic*. Their house had the typical farm kitchen with a Hoosier cabinet and shelves that held things like drying ears of corn, straw flowers, a *Dr. Miles Almanac* and a beekeeper's bonnet, bee smoker and hive tools. Behind the house they grew everything from "sparrow grass" to tobacco. They were frugal people who wasted nothing.

Having no children of their own, they were always glad to see us, and our visits were always rewarded with a hunk of Aunt Hannah's homemade bread smothered with comb honey. A big treat was one of her sugar cookies. They had the most interesting flavor, similar to popcorn.

After I graduated from high school I took over the chore of bread baking from my mother, and therefore considered myself a good enough baker to make some cookies from Aunt Hannah's recipe.

Try as I might, I could not get my cookies to have that *certain taste*. As frustrated as I was, I never mentioned it to my aunt until one day when I happened to be there as she was preparing to make them.

The flour and sugar were standard brands, the eggs were from the henhouse, and the baking powder

Aunt Hannah's Sugar Cookies

⅓ cup bacon grease (shortening)
1 cup sugar
2 eggs, beaten
1½ cups flour
1 tablespoon baking powder
½ teaspoon salt
1 teaspoon vanilla

Preheat oven to 425 degrees. Cream together shortening and sugar. Add eggs; beat well. Sift dry ingredients together and add to mixture with vanilla. Roll out about ¼-inch thick and cut into 3-inch rounds. Bake for about 8 minutes.

Facing page: 1955 French's Spices and Extracts ad, House of White Birches nostalgia archives and vanilla were from the A&P. The shorten-ing, however, was in a stoneware crock, and it looked like lard except that it had a grayish cast. I asked what it was.

"Smell it," she said.

One whiff told me what the secret ingredient was—bacon grease, which my thrifty aunt just could not bring herself to waste, but rendered for shortening. I should have known. ❖

Speaking of Cookies

By Colleen Heckenlively

A few days ago here in the Midwest, we had a blizzard, and as I almost always do, I headed for the kitchen to bake cookies. I don't know where the urge comes from, but when the weather turns bad, I feel the need to cook. Maybe it is the nesting instinct.

Anyway, I decided to make Girl Scout cookies from the original recipe. It is a simple cookie with simple ingredients, and as I mixed and stirred, my mind went back to my childhood and the cookies that my mother made most often.

She called them "tea cakes" and the ingredients were also simple: flour, sugar, shortening, milk, eggs, vanilla flavoring and a rising agent, either baking powder or baking soda.

Mother had a small table with an enamel top that she used for rolling out cookies, biscuits and piecrusts. She would sprinkle the top with flour, and after she had rolled the dough to the proper thickness, she would dip the rim of a drinking glass in granulated sugar and use that as a cutter.

Mother didn't have such a thing as a cookie sheet, so she used the pans in which she baked our biscuits and corn bread, what we today call a sheet-cake pan. She made very fat cookies and they were very good. We were a large family and very poor, but Mother was a good cook and could make a tasty meal out of whatever she had on hand.

Mother is 93 years old and in a nursing home now, and while frail of body, her mind is still sharp. We often talk about the Good Old Days—the big gardens she put in every summer, and the forays that she and we children made into the woods and fields.

We searched for anything we could find to put up for wintertime meals—wild grapes and muscadines for jams, jellies and juice, and apples from abandoned orchards for pies, jelly and just for eating.

Well, it is time to take my cookies out of the oven. Come on over for a visit and we will sample a few with a hot cup of coffee. ❖

───────⊷◉◈◉⊶───────

Original Girl Scout Cookies
This 1930s recipe was used for cookies sold in the Newton and Lexington area of Massachusetts.

1 cup butter
1 cup sugar
2 cups flour
½ teaspoon salt
2 teaspoons baking powder
2 eggs, beaten well
2 tablespoons milk
1 teaspoon vanilla

Cream butter and sugar together. Sift together flour, salt and baking powder. Add to creamed mixture along with the eggs, milk and vanilla. Mix well. Chill for about an hour.

Preheat oven to 425 degrees. Drop spoonfuls of dough onto ungreased baking sheet; flatten with bottom of drinking glass dipped in sugar. Bake for 8 to 10 minutes.

Toll House Original

By Jeanne M. Lesinski

*I*n 1930, Ken and Ruth Wakefield bought an old house in Whitman, Mass., some 20 miles from Boston. Ken, a former ship's steward, and Ruth, a registered dietician, wanted to own and operate a restaurant.

Ruth designed the menus and was the hostess, while Ken oversaw the kitchen of their Toll House restaurant, named for the old customs tollbooth that had once stood across the street.

One day Ruth was in a hurry to whip up a batch of cookies for that afternoon. She was in the middle of making them when she realized she didn't have the chopped nuts the recipe required.

Like everyone at the time, the Wakefields had to make do, so she chopped up a Nestlé chocolate bar and folded the pieces into the batter. She expected the chips to melt and make chocolate cookies. Instead, when she lifted the pan from the oven, she was surprised to find the chips intact. The cookie, which she dubbed the Toll House Chocolate Crunch Cookie, was delicious.

Both the Toll House cookie and the restaurant were an instant success. During World War II, the cookie's fame spread even farther when the Wakefields sent Toll House cookies to servicemen overseas.

Ruth died in 1977, and the Toll House burned to the ground seven years later. But her delectable cookies and Ruth's recipe (right) continue to excite the senses of young and old alike. ❖

Toll House cookie tin courtesy Barb Sprunger.

Toll House Chocolate Crunch Cookies

1 cup butter
¾ cup brown sugar
2 eggs, beaten
1 teaspoon hot water
1 teaspoon salt
2 packages semisweet chocolate morsels
1 teaspoon vanilla
¾ cup sugar
1 teaspoon baking soda
2¼ cups flour
1 cup chopped nuts

Preheat oven to 375 degrees. Grease cookie sheet. Cream butter. Add sugars and eggs; blend well. Dissolve baking soda in hot water. Sift flour and salt together. Add soda mixture to creamed mixture alternately with flour mixture. Stir in nuts, chocolate morsels and vanilla. Drop by half-teaspoonfuls onto prepared cookie sheet. Bake for 10 to 12 minutes. Makes 100 cookies.

At Toll House we chill this dough overnight. When ready for baking, we roll a teaspoon of dough between palms of hands and place balls 2 inches apart on greased baking sheets. Then we press balls with fingertips to form flat rounds. This keeps the cookies from spreading so much during baking and helps keep them uniformly round. They should be brown, though, and crispy, not white and hard as I have sometimes seen them.

The Sun-Maid Raisin Girl

By Jean E. Andrew

*I*n 1915, a young woman sat outside her home in Fresno, Calif., drying her hair in the midday sun. She never dreamed that a chance meeting that day would make her famous around the world as the Sun-Maid Raisin Girl. Grapes have been an important crop in California since the early 1800s, but no one thought of growing them especially for raisins until the summer of 1873, when a heat wave in the San Joaquin Valley shriveled the grapes on the vine.

The growers considered the whole crop a loss, but one man wasn't ready to face financial ruin without a fight. He loaded up his "dried grapes" and took them to San Francisco. (Evidently he'd never heard of raisins, although they had been around for thousands of years.) One shopkeeper agreed to try to sell them, and he put them out on the counter and called them "Peruvian Delicacies." They sold out in a few hours, and by the next day, other dealers were clamoring for more.

It was obvious that the growers were on to a good thing. The following year, grapes were picked and set in the sun to dry. The California raisin industry was on its way. By 1912, growers had joined forces as the California Associated Raisin Co.

When the Panama-Pacific International Exposition came to San Francisco in 1915, Lorraine Collett Petersen and several other girls who worked as packers for the raisin growers were sent to the exposition to hand out samples of raisins. Lorraine was thrilled when she was given the special job of going up in a small airplane every afternoon to drop a shower of raisins over the grounds of the exposition.

The Fresno Raisin Parade was important to the growers, so Lorraine was given time off from her job at the exposition to return home to take part in it. On the day of the parade, she wanted her hair to be just perfect, so she sat patiently while her mother twisted her long, dark hair into eight curls. To keep the curls in place, she put her mother's red sunbonnet on her head and sat out in the garden to enjoy the sun while her hair dried.

These raisins that you get *so cheaply* in the Sun-Maid bargain sacks

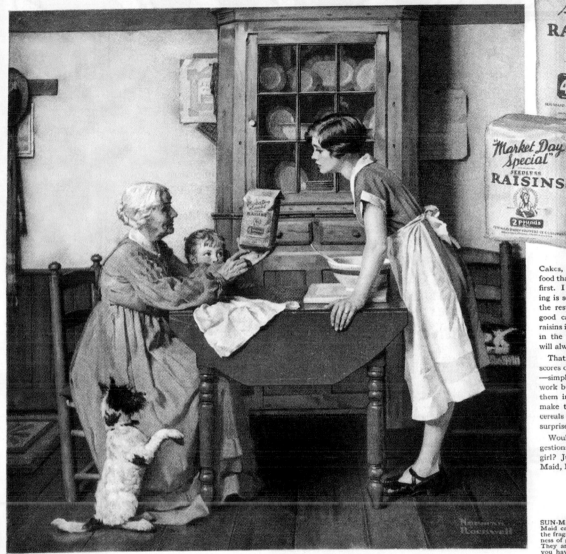

Cakes, somehow, seem to be the food that little cooks want to make first. I think I know why. Nothing is so apt to please daddy and the rest of the family as a real good cake. Especially one with raisins in the cake part and raisins in the frosting. Cakes like that will always be popular.

That, though, is just one of scores of ways to use these raisins—simple ways that mean no extra work but a lot better effect. Put them in plain puddings and you make them fancy. Put them in cereals and you have a breakfast surprise.

Would you like some other suggestions for yourself or your little girl? Just write me in care of Sun-Maid, Fresno, California.

Mary Dean

SUN-MAID NECTARS, in the red Sun-Maid carton, are seedless raisins with the fragrance, flavor and plump tenderness of grapes full ripened on the vine. They are like no other seedless raisins you have ever seen, a quality beyond compare.

SUN-MAID PUFFED, in the blue Sun-Maid carton, are seeded raisins that aren't sticky, the only seeded raisins that aren't sticky. And they hold *all* the flavor of the muscat grape. Your grocer has these two exclusive Sun-Maid products.

They make it easy to make things good

Beginner cooks learn it from their mothers or grandmothers; women hear it from their friends: The easiest way to make things good is to add good raisins. And thousands of women, now, name one kind of raisins—Sun-Maid's "Market Day Special" seedless.

They come in convenient bags of either 4 or 2 pounds, and the price is such that you *can* use them generously.

Quality hasn't been reduced a bit in these bargain Sun-Maid bags. Sun-Maid packs a tremendous volume of raisins—far more than anyone else. Special improved equipment does it economically. We have facilities for profitably disposing of raisins that are not perfectly fitted for your cooking. No one else does. So we can give you the biggest value for the money, and we do.

Try these raisins. Be sure you get the blue bag with the Sun-Maid girl on it.

GROWN AND PACKED BY **SUN-MAID** *Raisin Growers of California*   *A cooperative association of 17,000 individual growers*

An executive from the raisin company, Mr. Leroy Payne, was in town to see the parade with an official from the exposition and his wife. When he recognized Lorraine, he stopped to talk to her. The woman asked why she didn't wear the pretty red sunbonnet at their fair.

Lorraine laughed and answered, "I wasn't drying my hair then."

Lorraine forgot about the meeting until she returned to San Francisco and discovered that Mr. Payne had been so impressed by how attractive she looked in the red bonnet that he had convinced company officials to have all the girls wear red bonnets while they handed out raisin samples.

About that time, the company was trying to think of a trademark to put on its raisin boxes, and they discussed a logo showing a smiling girl gathering grapes in the sun. When Lorraine's name was mentioned, everyone agreed that she was just what they were looking for.

They hired an artist in San Francisco and sent Lorraine to sit for a portrait. For the next two weeks she sat for the artist in the morning and worked at the exposition in the afternoon. She was never paid to model for the picture, since the sittings were considered part of her regular job at the exposition, which paid $15 a week.

When Lorraine saw the finished portrait, she was thrilled with the striking picture of herself in the red sunbonnet, holding a tray of grapes, with a glowing yellow sunburst behind her. The portrait was exactly what the officials of the raisin company wanted, and it was approved as the official trademark of the California Associated Raisin Co., which was later renamed Sun-Maid Raisin Growers of California.

As the Sun-Maid Girl, Lorraine became a bit of a celebrity. She was asked to model clothes in stores and appear in booths at fairs. She was also given bit parts in several movies, including *The Trail of the Lonesome Pine*, and one company put out Sun-Maid Girl dolls. As her face became more familiar, she began to receive letters from all over the world.

Lorraine was a remarkable woman who went on to run a cattle-breeding ranch. She also became a nurse and operated a convalescent home for many years. Her portrait, which had been given to her by the company, hung in the hallway of the rest home for many years, and later in her own home. Even when she was older, she still enjoyed making appearances on television as the one and only Sun-Maid Girl.

Before she passed away in 1983 at the age of 90, Mrs. Petersen presented the original portrait and her old red bonnet to the president of the Sun-Maid Growers of California. The portrait now hangs in a place of honor in the Sun-Maid factory in Kingsburg, Calif., and the faded red bonnet is displayed in a glass case nearby.

The Sun-Maid logo has been updated over the years, but it is still based on the portrait of Lorraine holding the tray of grapes, with the glowing sunburst behind her.

Although few people are familiar with her name, Lorraine Collett Petersen's image is one of the best-known trademarks in the world. ❖

Sun-Maid Raisin Cookies

1 cup sugar
1 cup shortening
½ cup milk
2 cups rolled oats
½ teaspoon salt
2 cups flour

2 eggs
1½ cups raisins
2 teaspoons baking powder
½ teaspoon soda
1½ teaspoons lemon extract

Plunge raisins into hot water for a minute and drain. Cream shortening with sugar, then add beaten eggs and milk. Add rolled oats, beat well, then add flour sifted with baking powder, soda and salt. When thoroughly mixed, add raisins and lemon extract. Drop in small portions on a greased baking sheet and bake about 12 minutes in a moderate oven (350 degrees).

Air Raids & Raisin Pie

By Patrick Malone

Mom baked all sorts of good things back before plastic wrap and machine-made doughnuts. In the early 1940s, however, her wonderful pies and cakes became scarce creations, as many of the essential ingredients were rationed.

Eating Mom's raisin pie was a pastime that ranked above sucking on cherry Popsicles.

Of course, eating didn't meet all of an 8-year-old's demands, and our little town seemed a pretty unthrilling place to live.

Summer days were passed playing softball with friends, hiking in the woods and going to movies. There wasn't a whole lot else to do—until the government decided that the residents of our community had best be prepared in case of a real emergency. We then became acquainted with air-raid drills.

One summer night, when the sun had been down for nearly half an hour, my friend Donald and I were playing in new-mown grass and trying to ignore the hordes of mosquitoes. Suddenly the sirens wailed. We headed for my house as fast as our legs could carry us.

In the excitement of the moment, I forgot that Mother had finally found time to make my favorite dessert just before I had gone out to play. Had I remembered,

The bad news: Donald had stepped into the middle of the pie.

I would have also recalled where she invariably placed her pies to cool. Donald and I dashed up to our front porch and took a shortcut behind the old, creaky swing, toward the dark doorway to our living room. Just as the siren ran out of breath and before it could howl again, I heard Donald exclaim, "Oh, m'gosh!"

There was bad news and good news. The bad news was that Donald had indeed stepped directly into the middle of the pie. The good news was that Donald had a very small foot, and the German bombers didn't show up that night.

When the lights went back on, we all gave thanks with an unusual raisin pie—one with the center cut out. Even Donald got a piece.

It wouldn't be long before sirens squealed and church bells pealed to celebrate victory. The entire neighborhood hugged and kissed and danced in the streets. The years would fly by and fade into tattered, hazy nostalgia, but one thing was certain: Nobody in our family would ever eat a piece of raisin pie again without remembering Donald, the sirens, the fear, and the hope. ❖

Raisin Pie

1 cup seedless raisins
2 cups cider or water
½ cup brown sugar
½ teaspoon cinnamon
⅛ teaspoon ground cloves
2 tablespoons butter
½ cup chopped nuts
4 tablespoons cornstarch

1 tablespoon coriander (optional)
⅛ teaspoon salt
⅛ teaspoon nutmeg
2 tablespoons lemon juice
1 cup sugar
Pastry for 2-crust pie

Heat oven to 350 degrees. Combine raisins and cider in a medium saucepan. Bring to a boil; boil for 2 or 3 minutes, stirring occasionally. Add brown sugar, coriander, cinnamon, salt, cloves, nutmeg, butter, lemon juice and nuts to mixture in saucepan. In small bowl, combine sugar and cornstarch. Add to hot raisin mixture and boil until thick, stirring constantly. Line pie pan with pastry. Pour in raisin filling and top with top crust. Bake until crust is done. Serve hot.

Shoo-Fly Pie

By Lucy Tharp

My father, General Davenport, was a master molasses maker. No, "General" was not a military title; it was Dad's Christian name. He cooked sorghum molasses in the old-fashioned, traditional way. We lived on a farm in the Chestnut Hill community in Cumberland County, Tenn. Dad owned the only molasses mill in the area.

During late summer and early fall, he traveled around to different communities with it. Sometimes he was away from home for weeks at a stretch, staying overnight at the home where he was making molasses at the time. Dad used to joke, "If you want to be a man of the world, just travel with a sorghum mill."

Once Dad had his mill set up and ready to operate, the farmer would cut his sorghum cane and bring it to the mill site. The cane was passed through large rollers called "crushers," which mashed the juice from the stalks. A mule powered the mill. It was hitched to a long pole that was fastened to a shaft, which in turn moved the rollers as the mule walked continuously around the apparatus in a wide circle.

The raw cane juice was caught in a large barrel with a pipe in the bottom. Through the pipe, the juice was siphoned off into a flat, 12-foot pan. The juice was then heated over a wood fire that had been placed under the pan in a furnace made of brick.

It was called shoo-fly pie because flies had to be shooed away.

The big pan was of a unique design. It had dividers all the way down it from one end to the other. The first divider extended from the right side of the pan to a point about 2 inches from the left side. The next divider began on the left side and extended across the pan to within about 2 inches of the right side.

The pan was filled with these dividers, alternating from one side to the other, creating a long pathway back and forth across the pan and down it from one end to the other.

By the time the juice had wound its way, serpentine fashion, to the end of the pan, it had cooked and could be siphoned off as syrup. Dad occasionally used a wooden paddle to aid the flow of boiling cane juice in its journey through the pan.

Seven to 10 gallons of raw cane juice boiled down to 1 gallon of molasses. All refuse and waste came to the top as the juice cooked. Dad removed it with a skimmer—a fine wire sieve attached to a long handle.

It took about an hour to cook a batch of juice in this fashion. The new syrup was drawn off and placed in large containers to cool before it was poured into jars.

Cane juice, however, provided more than just molasses for human consumption. The juice, rich in sugar, could be made into a thick nectar over a period of about two weeks.

By suspending a coarse twine string from a cork and inserting the cork in the mouth of a quart jar, rock candy could be formed. The juice was 10 percent sugar, and it crystallized around the string, forming rock candy, which was easily removed from the jar and the cork. It was not uncommon for some families to use this rock candy for cooking.

The byproducts of the cane also had practical uses. The pulp was stored to be used as cattle feed in the winter. The waste skimmings were often saved and used for hot feed.

Freshly cooked molasses was always a treat. I remember the anticipation on a cold winter morning of sitting down to a breakfast of fresh pork, home-churned butter and hot biscuits topped with fresh sorghum molasses. What a treat!

I suppose, however, that my most pleasant memories of molasses are prompted by a most delicious but simple dessert my mother made from molasses. It was called shoo-fly pie. She explained that the pie was called shoo-fly from the idea that flies attracted by the molasses had to be shooed away.

This is her recipe for shoo-fly pie. I still bake this pie using this recipe, especially during the winter months.

Shoo-Fly Pie

1 cup molasses
2 eggs, beaten
1 teaspoon baking soda
1½ cups hot water
1½ cups flour
1 cup brown sugar
1 teaspoon salt
1 teaspoon cinnamon
¼ teaspoon ground ginger
¼ teaspoon nutmeg
4 tablespoons butter
2 (9-inch) unbaked,
    single-crust pie shells
Whipped cream or ice cream

Preheat oven to 350 degrees. Combine molasses, eggs, baking soda and hot water. Mix well. Pour into unbaked pie shells.

Combine flour, brown sugar, salt, cinnamon, ginger, nutmeg and butter. Mix to a crumbly consistency. Sprinkle crumb mixture over tops of pies. Bake for 10 minutes, or until fork inserted in pies comes out clean. Makes 2 (9-inch) pies.

Top each slice with a generous dollop of whipped cream. Shoo-fly pie is also delicious with a scoop of ice cream.

Our forefathers worked hard, long hours on their farms. Eating was one of the few pleasures they could look forward to. They made the best of every meal.

From the 1930s through the mid-1950s, Dad practiced his old-time art of cooking sorghum molasses. He traveled with his mill around several Middle Tennessee counties, including Putnam, White, Roane, Bledsoe and Fentress, as well as Cumberland County, where we lived.

Dad's last year as a sorghum chef was 1955. He was getting on in years and the mill was becoming more and more difficult to maintain.

Also, with each passing year, fewer farmers were growing sorghum cane. Dad summed it up when he said, "People don't want to stay at home and raise cane anymore. They'd rather go to town and raise Cain on Saturday nights." ❖

Mock Apple Pie
I have made this Ritz cracker recipe from the 1940s many times and have been asked what kind of apples I used.

Pastry for 9-inch 2-crust pie
36 Ritz crackers, coarsely broken
   (about 1¾ cups crumbs)
2 cups water
2 cups sugar
2 teaspoons cream of tartar
2 tablespoons lemon juice
Grated peel of 1 lemon
2 tablespoons butter or margarine
   ½ teaspoon cinnamon

Line 9-inch pie plate with one layer of pastry; place crackers in prepared crust. In saucepan over high heat, heat water, sugar and cream of tartar to a boil.

Simmer for 15 minutes. Add lemon juice and grated peel. Let cool.

Preheat oven to 425 degrees. Pour cooled syrup over crackers.

Dot with butter; sprinkle with cinnamon. Place top crust over pie; seal and flute edges.

Cut slits in top crust to allow steam to escape. Bake for 30 to 35 minutes, or until crust is crispy and golden.

Cool completely before serving. Serves 8.

—*Hazel M. Kennison*

1930 Kalamazoo stove ad; House of White Birches nostalgia archives

Gooseberry Pie

By Laurie Kolesnick

Gooseberry pie was my grand-mother's specialty and something I have never forgotten. I sat on a small stool, watching my grand-mother as she made her pie. She kept a small pile of flour at the side of the breadboard, and other items for the dough—lard, salt and a little water—sat in front of her. She mixed just so much of everything. Then, using a dusting from the flour pile, she rolled the dough into a circle just the right size for the pie shell.

Her pie was baked to a golden brown and bubbled as she brought it out from the black woodstove heated by wood and coal.

The cabinet Grandmother worked on was equipped with a flour sifter above the bread-board. Behind the mirrored doors at the top was a pull-out bin that held 50 pounds of flour. She had everything at her fingertips whenever she baked. She told me, "Honey, when you are worried over something and maybe times seem extra hard, or maybe you have company coming, bake a gooseberry pie. It will be a special surprise to everyone and will also help rid your mind of troubles."

Every time my husband and I have moved, we have taken our gooseberry plants with us. My grandmother's words have never left me, and all the plants have grown, with huge berries. We have never lost a bush. Here is Grandma's Gooseberry pie recipe, along with another reci-pe I have used. ❖

Grandma's Recipe

4 cups fresh gooseberries
1 cup or more sugar
½ teaspoon cinnamon
2 tablespoons butter
Pastry for 2-crust pie

Mix all ingredients except pastry and let stand for 15 minutes. Preheat oven to 350 degrees. Line pie plate with pastry. Add filling; top with top crust. Bake for 45 minutes.

Gooseberry Pie

3 cups gooseberries
1½ cups sugar, divided
¼ cup water
3 tablespoons quick-cooking tapioca
Dash of salt
½ teaspoon cinnamon
½ teaspoon ground cloves
⅛ teaspoon nutmeg
Butter
Pastry for 2-crust pie
Marshmallows

Combine gooseberries, 1 cup sugar and water; cook until gooseberries are tender. Set aside.

Mix ½ cup sugar, tapioca, salt, cinnamon, cloves and nutmeg. Stir into cooked fruit; cool.

Heat oven to 450 degrees. Line a 9-inch pie plate with pastry. Fill with fruit mixture, dot with butter, and arrange pastry strips in lattice pattern over top. Bake for 10 minutes.

Reduce heat to 350 degrees and bake for 20 longer. When almost brown, remove from oven. Place a marshmallow in each diamond-shaped opening; return pie to oven to finish browning.

Wild Blackberry Cobbler

By Glenn Herndon

Wild blackberry vines have been seeded in by the birds and now grow rank between my neighbor's property and mine. This spring a long branch reached out into one of my best rose bushes, and I knew I had to remove it or have a bigger mess later on. Foolishly, using an ungloved hand, I reached out and took the tip of the vines between my thumb and forefinger. Fine, barely visible thorns grabbed my skin and would not let go without bringing blood.

I realized then what Mother had put me through those many years ago in the Good Old Days, when I was a big boy of 7 and was learning to help out around our place in Oklahoma.

My older brothers had discovered a great expanse of wild blackberry vines in the creek bottom adjacent to several acres of other bottomland we had rented in hopes of growing bountiful harvests of corn.

As soon as the blackberries were ripe, Mother said she and I would harvest all we could for canning for winter pies. She put on her old-fashioned sunbonnet and an old, long-sleeved dress, and I dressed in bib overalls and long-sleeved shirt with a straw hat. Every morning after breakfast we headed for the blackberry patch.

"I declare, you are a sight from eating all those berries! You are purple all around your mouth!"

My experiences in the blackberry patch made 1936 the most memorable year for me. I immediately found the vines to be horrible to work around. They didn't want to give up their fruit easily; they fought back with vicious thorns that tore into my skin through my shirt.

Eventually I learned to pluck the berries gingerly and avoid the thorns. The berries were vine-ripened, and they had a marvelous flavor. I ate as many as I put in my bucket.

But it was hot in that creek bottom, and I grumped, "When will this be over? We just pick, pick, PICK!"

Mother just laughed. "You don't know how to work yet!" she exclaimed. "And no wonder your bucket isn't filling up very fast. I declare, you are a sight from eating all those berries! You are purple all around your mouth!"

However, each day we eventually filled our two buckets and went home to can the berries. I pumped water for the washtubs and brought wood for the old stove my brothers and Dad had set up under a brush arbor out in the yard to provide Mother with shade while she canned.

And each day, until the berries were gone, she put up five or six quarts. She made a few pies and promised we'd get more in the winter, when fruit for pies was scarce.

When winter came, she began using the berries we had harvested. She topped off her cobbler servings with big dollops of whipped cream courtesy of Daisy, our Jersey cow. Such good memories of the rewards of our labor cancel out the bad memories of the thorny vines.

She told my brothers that she could not have done it without my help.

"Why, he never complained once!" she said.

My brothers did not answer, but oh, the dirty

Co-editor Janice Tate made this delicious blackberry cobbler from Glenn's mother's recipe for her husband, Ken. Photograph by Janice Tate.

looks they gave me! They knew better!

Below is Mother's recipe—or, as she would have said, her "receipt"—for wild blackberry cobbler. (It is fine with tame ones, too.)

The recipe is identical to my mother's except that she would have used lard for the pastry.

I received this recipe from Roberta Newton of Boyd, Texas, which is not far from where we lived when I helped Mother gather blackberries. ❖

Wild Blackberry Cobbler

Filling:
1 quart blackberries
½ cup sugar
3 tablespoons butter

1 cup water
2 tablespoons cornstarch

Crust:
1½ cups flour
¼ cup cold water
½ cup butter-flavored vegetable shortening

1 teaspoon salt
Sugar for sprinkling

For filling, combine blackberries, water, sugar and cornstarch in a heavy medium saucepan. Cook the filling over medium heat while you make the crust, stirring it occasionally. Mixture will thicken.

For crust, combine flour and salt. Cut in shortening using pastry blender or two knives until it is like coarse cornmeal. Add cold water. Knead dough lightly, then roll out. Work the dough quickly and lightly; the more you work it, the tougher it will become.

Preheat oven to 400 degrees. Cut crust to fit in bottom of a 9 x 13-inch pan; place in pan. Pour in filling. Cut strips from remaining dough for lattice top. Cut any remaining dough into small pieces; push them down into blackberry filling, to cook like dumplings as cobbler bakes.

Dot surface of filling with small pieces of butter. Put on lattice top; sprinkle with sugar. Bake for 20 to 25 minutes.

Green Tomato Pie

By Ann Casper as told to Jeannie Moore

*I*n the summer of 1944 I was only 5 and full of mischief. My parents had a garden with green tomatoes, okra, cucumbers and many other vegetables. I watched my father pick the tomatoes and give them to my mother. She always smiled and thanked him for bringing in fresh vegetables. Often she would kiss him for the work he had done.

I loved my mother's smiles because her eyes seemed to twinkle and her face would light up. I wanted my mother to give me the same smile she gave Dad.

I took a bucket outside with me to the garden. I eagerly picked both red and green tomatoes until the bucket was full. As I picked, I would eat some of the juicy red tomatoes. My shirt soon was soaked with tomato juice dripping down the front. The more I picked, the sleepier I seemed to get. I soon lay down on the ground and went to sleep.

At some point Mom started looking for the bucket. She looked through the house and out in the front yard and then in the back yard. Then she started to panic when she realized that she did not know where I was. She went to the barn and started having my father look for me. "Ann, Ann!" they called. "Where are you?" The more they yelled, the more Mom worried.

Dad asked, "Have you looked in the garden?"

"No," she answered. They both walked quickly to the garden and found me there, sound asleep. Then they saw the bucket of tomatoes, ripe ones and green ones, and my shirt soaked with tomato juice.

"Ann, what have you been doing?" yelled my mother.

"Mommy, I wanted to surprise you with fresh tomatoes so you would smile at me the way you do Dad," I explained. Then I started crying because I thought they were angry with me.

"Ann, come here," Dad said. "I am happy that you tried to help, but tomatoes don't get picked until they are ripe and red," he explained.

Tears in her eyes, Mom smiled and said, "Ann, I am proud of you for trying, but the water bucket is for water. Green tomatoes do not get picked unless I use them for a special recipe. What if I made us a green tomato pie?"

I looked at Mom and gave her a hug. My mother was smiling at me with her eyes twinkling, just like she did at my dad.

Mom and Dad always loved to tease me about the day I picked green and ripe tomatoes. These memories are precious to me. ❖

Mom's Green Tomato Pie

Pastry for a 2-crust, 9-inch pie
½ cup of sugar or a little more
2 tablespoons flour
Grated peel of 1 lemon
Grated peel of 1 orange
¼ teaspoon ground allspice
¼ teaspoon salt
4 to 4½ green tomatoes, peeled
    and sliced
1 tablespoon lemon juice
1 tablespoon orange juice
3 tablespoons butter

Preheat oven to 350 degrees. Line pie pan with pastry for bottom crust.

Mix the sugar, flour, lemon peel, orange peel, allspice and salt. Sprinkle just a little of the mixture in the bottom of the pie shell.

Arrange the green tomato slices in pie shell, one layer at a time. Cover each layer of tomatoes with sugar mixture; then sprinkle it with lemon and orange juices, and dot it with butter.

Keep adding layers until you reach the top of the pie tin, then cover with top crust.

Bake for 45 to 60 minutes.

"Like mother used to make"

Mincemeat Pie

4 medium apples, peeled, cored
   and finely chopped
¼ pound raisins, seeded, seedless
   or a combination
¼ pound dried cranberries
¼ pound mixed dried fruit, minced
¼ cup chopped or candied orange peel
¼ pound lean beef, ground
⅛ pound suet, ground
½ cup cider
½ cup water
⅛ cup nuts (walnuts, pecans, etc.)
⅓ cup sugar, brown sugar or molasses
¼ teaspoon cinnamon
¼ teaspoon mace
¼ teaspoon ground cloves
Dash nutmeg
Dash salt
Dash pepper

Mix all ingredients thoroughly. Place in a large pot and cook at medium-low temperature for 2 hours, stirring frequently. Remove to large bowl; cool and refrigerate or freeze until used. Makes enough for 2 pies.

—Dr. Allen H. Benton

Peanut Butter Pie

4 ounces cream cheese
¾ cup peanut butter
1 cup confectioners' sugar

½ cup milk
1 teaspoon vanilla
8 ounces whipped topping
Graham-cracker piecrust

Using electric mixer, blend cream cheese, peanut butter, confectioners' sugar, milk and vanilla. Fold in whipped topping. Pour into graham-cracker crust. Freeze for 4 to 6 hours, or overnight. Let stand at room temperature for 15–20 minutes before serving.

Sweet Potato Pie

16 ounces mashed cooked
   sweet potatoes
1 can sweetened condensed milk
2 eggs, beaten
1 teaspoon vanilla
1 teaspoon cinnamon
½ teaspoon nutmeg
9-inch unbaked pie shell

Preheat oven to 425 degrees. Beat sweet potatoes, sweetened condensed milk, eggs, vanilla, cinnamon and nutmeg until well blended. Pour into pie shell. Bake for 15 minutes.

Reduce heat to 350 degrees and bake for 30 minutes more.

—Jackie Maue

Shake Them 'Simmons Down

By Jamie Fields

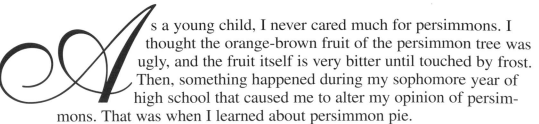s a young child, I never cared much for persimmons. I thought the orange-brown fruit of the persimmon tree was ugly, and the fruit itself is very bitter until touched by frost. Then, something happened during my sophomore year of high school that caused me to alter my opinion of persimmons. That was when I learned about persimmon pie.

Miss Hopkins, our home-economics teacher, decided to have a pie contest—but it would be different from usual pie contests. Our entries would be judged not only on taste and eye appeal, but also on their uniqueness. Simply put, the pie had to be good eating *and* above the ordinary. The high school basketball squad would act as the judges.

"Ugh!" I exclaimed. "Persimmons?
Those bitter, sour things?"

I liked several of the boys on the squad, so I was especially interested in making a good impression.

But something else motivated me to make a good showing. That "something" was Jane Wesley.

Jane was the epitome of the spoiled brat. She was an only child, and from the day of her birth, her parents had pampered her and provided her with the most expensive toys and clothing.

As soon as she learned about the contest, she made it clear that she intended to win. "My pie will be very unusual," she declared. "I'll go to the store and get the most exotic ingredients money can buy. I'm not about to go out stumbling through briar patches, hunting berries."

I, too, was determined to win. But reality started to set in. I had to admit that our pantry had a limited stock of supplies. Mom had canned apples, peaches and blackberries, but they were far from unique.

The next day was Saturday, and that morning I went to Mom for advice. "Why don't you talk to your Grandma Winnie?" she suggested. This was sound advice indeed. My Grandma Winnie Davenport had grown up in an era when people had to make do with whatever resources were available. Grandma Winnie's root cellar was well-stocked with canned fruits, vegetables and dried herbs. I walked over to Grandma's house and told her about my problem.

"Well, persimmons are coming in season," she said. "They make beautiful pies, and they are delicious."

"Ugh!" I exclaimed. "Persimmons? Those bitter, sour things?"

"Frost takes all that away." She chuckled. "When is this big pie contest taking place?"

"Next Friday afternoon," I replied.

"Well, don't worry," she assured me. "By the middle of the week, persimmons should be just right for picking. I'll go out Thursday morning and pick some windfalls. Those will be the riper ones. I'll bring them over to your house when you get home from school and I'll show you how to make a pie that no store-bought pie can match for taste *or* looks."

The following Thursday afternoon, when I got off the school bus, Grandma was right on schedule with a gallon can full of persimmons. First we washed and peeled the persimmons. Then we pressed the fruit through a colander. With Grandma's coaching, I added the other ingredients and cooked the filling in a double boiler. After I poured the cooked filling into a baked shell, I topped it with frothy meringue.

Some of the filling was left in the saucepan. When I tasted it, I found it to be rich in taste, and smooth and creamy in texture. It was indeed a beautiful pie.

The judging table was set up in the home-economics room. The table was filled end to end with an array of delectable but unidentified pies. Neither the name of the pie nor its ingredients were to be revealed before the judging. Yet I was astounded to overhear Jane Wesley talking to some of the judges about her pie.

"My pie is a closely guarded recipe," she said. "Just last summer when we went to Florida, Mother and I ate in this very exclusive restaurant. We ordered the key lime pie and we enjoyed it so much that we asked the waiter for the recipe. He said he couldn't give it to us because it was a house secret. We got the recipe by slipping the waiter a 10-spot. It was well worth it, but I did have a hard time getting all the ingredients. We had to go all the way to Knoxville to get those special key limes."

In despair, I looked at Jane's pie. It was tantalizing. It made my mouth water just to look at it. I resigned myself to losing. The judging began. We sat and watched patiently as members of the basketball squad cut and tasted the pies. When the judging ended, Mr. Sizemore, our principal, started to announce the winners in his loud, stentorian voice. "Third place goes to Edna Warren for her honey-cheese pie." A round of applause followed.

"Second prize goes to Glenda Young for her buttermilk cream pie." More applause. I sat, my eyes closed, waiting for the inevitable.

"And the first-place blue ribbon winner is …" Mrs. Sizemore paused for effect. "… Jamie Livesay, for her persimmon meringue pie."

I thought I was going to faint. Several of the girls hugged and congratulated me. Even Jane shook my hand. She tried to smile, but her features were hard and strained. "You had a beautiful pie, Jane," I said as I hugged her.

"Well, you surprised me," she said, trying to conceal her disappointment. "I just didn't expect you to go to the woods and rob a poor old 'possum of its dinner."

I was not angry with Jane. On the contrary, I felt compassion for her. Her attitude brought to mind a passage of Scripture my mother often read from Ecclesiastes: "All is vanity."

After all these years I still enjoy persimmon pies. I'd like to share Grandma Winnie's persimmon meringue pie recipe with you. ❖

Persimmon Meringue Pie

Enough sweet, very ripe persimmons to make 2 cups pulp	
½ cup sugar	2 egg yolks
½ teaspoon ground or grated nutmeg	Baked pastry shell
¼ teaspoon salt	2 teaspoons butter
	1 teaspoon grated lemon peel
	Meringue

Peel persimmons. Press through a colander to make 2 cups pulp. Add sugar, nutmeg, lemon peel and salt. Cook slowly for 5 minutes.

Blend a small amount of the hot mixture into butter and broken egg yolks; return all to persimmon mixture and stir until slightly thickened.

Pour persimmon mixture into pastry shell and cover with meringue. Bake for 10 minutes, or until meringue is browned. As an option, let pie cool and top with whipped topping. Garnish with maraschino cherries. Makes 1 (9-inch) pie.

The Noon Hour Was Dinnertime

Chapter Three

*D*inner time!" That was Mama's call every day around the noon hour. When did the midday meal cease being dinner? I don't know, but any kid from the Good Old Days will tell you that supper was the evening meal. The noon hour was dinnertime.

The favorite dinner meal of my youth had to be that ubiquitous, all-American institution called Sunday dinner. In the Tate household, Sunday dinner followed church and could be held one of two ways.

The first was when we loaded up into our old car and drove the four or five miles to my grandparents' home. Grandma and Grandpa Tate were the center of a Sunday dinner tradition that almost always included several of their 11 children and at least a couple of dozen grandchildren. I would guess 80 percent of our Sunday dinners were spent connecting the dots generationally from grandparent to parent to child to cousin to aunt and uncle.

But far and away my favorite way to spend my favorite meals was the few times we had cookouts. Whether it was at a campground or recreation area or just in the front yard of our simple home, I came to love those outdoor dinners. Hamburgers and hotdogs taste better when licked by the heat of an open grill.

Mama's potato salad, baked beans and strawberry shortcake for dessert rounded out the meal, fueling young bodies for a long afternoon of Hide and Seek and Follow the Leader.

Today I still love cookouts, possibly because now Janice and I are the focus of the younger generations. We gather as often as we can on the old home place and I fire up the old grill. I have yet to relinquish my apron and utensils, but the day is probably coming. Meanwhile, I enjoy warm summer Sunday afternoons and the memories of when the noon hour was dinnertime back in the Good Old Days.

—Ken Tate

Janice's Potato Salad

My dear wife's potato salad is a family favorite for our cookouts. Her secret ingredient is the dilled green tomato relish, that she still cans from our garden each year. I prefer to eat Janice's potato salad while it is still warm.

4 medium potatoes, peeled, diced and boiled
4 green onions, sliced (about ½ cup)
¾ cup dill green tomato relish (my favorite) or dill pickle relish
2 tablespoons prepared dijon mustard
½ cup mayonnaise
½ teaspoon salt
¼ teaspoon pepper
6 hard-boiled eggs (4 chopped, 2 sliced for garnish)

Combine all ingredients except 2 sliced eggs in large bowl and mix well. Place sliced eggs for garnish on top. Refrigerate and serve. Makes 6 servings.

Corned-Beef Soup

By Helen Bradfield Shambaugh

During the late 1930s and 1940s, my parents, siblings and I lived on an apple orchard in Morgan County, W.Va. Our home, owned by the orchard company for which our father worked, was an old log house. It had been built long before by some other family. My older sister was married and gone, and my younger sister had not been born yet, so I was the only girl, along with my four brothers.

From our gardens, in which the whole family worked, we harvested potatoes and other vegetables. These, along with the ground-fallen fruit, which the orchard owners allowed us to gather, kept us from ever being hungry. We canned everything we could; we stored cabbages, potatoes and apples in our root cellar; and we made jams, jellies and apple butter.

Our chickens supplied us with eggs and meat. We butchered a couple of hogs in the fall, and our father hunted squirrels, turkeys and rabbits to supplement our simple fare. We ate a lot of dried beans, cornmeal mush and skillet gravy. With "a pinch of this and a handful of that," our mother could make a good-tasting, nourishing meal.

How could she put so much flavor in that big kettle of soup?

One dish that I remember well is Mom's vegetable soup. Sometimes she used a ham bone or some bacon fat or ham fryings to season the broth. We could not afford to buy regular beef for soup, but sometimes Mom would buy a can of corned beef. It made the best soup of all.

I remember coming up the path to the back of our house and being welcomed by the aromas of that corned-beef soup and Mom's home-made bread wafting through the old screened door. I waited eagerly until the food was ready.

Like many other women of Appalachia, Mom had taught herself to season things deliciously to make simple food tasty. How she could put so much flavor in that big kettle of soup with just one can of corned beef, I will never know.

I am now a 70-year-old widow, and though I am not wealthy, I can afford to buy beef for making soup. Still, every so often, I get a craving for corned-beef soup with homemade bread. Even though my soup never does seem to taste quite as good as my mother's did, I enjoy eating it.

If you ever pass my door and catch the aromas of soup cooking and bread baking, stop in. We'll sit and visit and talk about the Good Old Days until the victuals are ready. Then we'll enjoy them together—just as we did during the Depression years.

Give them GOOD HOT SOUP FOR LUNCH

Every day, 27 million people share this happy eating habit!

America loves soup for lunch—that's what a nation-wide survey shows! And these wintry days, good hot soup for lunch is a *special* favorite. For soup is a grand food . . . delicious . . . nourishing . . . easy to digest . . . easy to serve. (Just 4 minutes from stove to table.) It's thrifty—an outstanding food value. And variety . . . 21 Campbell's kinds to choose from . . . a soup for every menu and every taste. So *today*—every day—have soup for lunch!

SOUP, SANDWICH AND DESSERT   Campbell's Chicken Noodle Soup

Pieces of plump, tender chicken . . . mingled with golden egg noodles in gleaming broth! An old Colonial favorite.

Cream cheese & olive sandwich   Milk   Gingerbread

SOUP AND DESSERT   Campbell's Beef Soup

Generous pieces of tender beef and plenty of hearty vegetables . . . mingled in thick brown beef stock! Grand good eating!

Applesauce with whipped cream   Coffee

SOUP AND SALAD   Campbell's Green Pea Soup

A velvety-smooth purée of choice green peas blended with fine table butter. High in nourishment—and delicious!

Waldorf Salad   Tea   Cheese Biscuits

Oh, would you like the recipe for the soup? How my late mother would chuckle! "Lands!" she would say. "I never use a recipe. I just put in whatever I happen to have on hand."

However, I can try to tell you how you might get started. Just remember: All the measurements are approximate, and what you add or leave out is up to you. I'm betting you will like it. ❖

Corned-Beef Vegetable Soup

3 or 4 large potatoes, peeled and diced
1 medium onion, chopped
3 or 4 cups chopped cabbage
Water
Salt, pepper and other seasonings
    to taste
1 can corned beef, crumbled
    (or more, as desired)
16-ounce can whole kernel corn,
    undrained
2 pounds frozen mixed vegetables,
    or equivalent amount of
    canned and/or fresh
    vegetables, including
    carrots, peas, okra, celery,
    green beans, squash,etc.
1 pint crushed tomatoes or
    tomato juice

Into a large soup pot, place potatoes, onion and cabbage. Add water to cover the vegetables by a couple of inches; place pot over medium heat. Add salt, pepper and other seasonings to taste. Add corned beef.

Stir in canned corn with its liquid. You may substitute frozen or fresh corn, but canned corn adds unique flavor. Stir. Bring to a boil, then reduce heat and cook until potatoes are tender.

Add frozen, canned and/or fresh vegetables. Stir in tomatoes or juice, using more or less according to your taste. Cook slowly.

Mom would simmer this all day on the back of her woodburning cookstove. Not many of us have a woodstove available nowadays, so just cook slowly until all the vegetables are tender, giving it a good stir now and then.

Add more liquid as desired or needed, always remembering to adjust seasonings when adding anything. The way to do this is to keep tasting, as any good cook will tell you.

Eat when it tastes like it's ready. Warming any leftover soup only makes it better.

Of course, cooked in this manner, each kettle of soup will be a little different, but in the days of "make do," that's just the way it was.

Happy eating!

Is It or Isn't It Stew?

By Aline Soukup

My daughter was puzzled when a friend reminisced about the good stew she had eaten at my daughter's house, for she seldom cooks stew. She then remembered that I cook some of her family's favorite meals, which she stores in her freezer. It was one of these meals, my special recipe for chuck roast, that her friend thought was stew.

Having relished chuck roast many times at my mother-in-law's house, I made it a point to learn how she cooked it when I married her son. I used the same ingredients she did, but I cooked and served it differently.

My mother-in-law roasted the chuck in a roasting pan with whole carrots and potatoes surrounding it, plus chopped onion, green pepper and a tomato.

When the meat was done, she made a lot of gravy from the drippings, and after cutting the roast into small serving pieces and removing all the fat and gristle, she put the meat back into the gravy and served it as a stew.

I cooked chuck roast that way until I received a pressure cooker as a Christmas gift. Since pressure cooking does wonders for low-grade cuts of meat, I experimented with chuck roast in the cooker; as a result of those experiments, I cook it no other way.

I cut the roast into serving pieces and trim the fat and gristle away *before cooking.*

This is a tedious job if you don't have a sharp knife. I brown these chunks of meat in the pressure cooker; add water to cover; add chopped onion, green pepper and tomato sauce; and then cook it for 25 minutes. Meanwhile, I cook small-to-medium carrot pieces in another pressure cooker for 3 minutes.

When the meat is done, I add the carrot water to the liquid in the pot, bring it to a boil, and thicken it with a flour-and-water mixture. When the meat and carrots are added to the gravy, My Way Chuck Roast (or Stew) is ready to be served over mashed potatoes. If there are leftovers, my family eats it over bread in place of potatoes.

As a rule, chuck is stringy. But when cooked in the pressure cooker, it turns out so tender, one hardly notices the stringiness. However, since there is a lot of waste with chuck when you cut away all the gristle and fat, if I can't find a good cut of chuck, I buy London broil, which has little waste. Also, if pressed for time, I use lean, ready-cut stew meat. ❖

My Way Chuck Roast (or Stew)

1 (3- to 5-pound) chuck roast
Water
1 medium onion, chopped
1 medium green pepper, chopped
1 small can tomato sauce
1 package carrots, cut into pieces
Flour
Hot mashed potatoes

Use a sharp knife to cut roast into serving pieces and remove gristle and fat. Brown meat in pressure cooker and cover with water. Add chopped onion, green pepper and tomato sauce. (A fresh, chopped tomato may be substituted.) Cook for 25 minutes in pressure cooker.

In the meantime, cook carrots in another pressure cooker for 3 minutes. Carrots may be cooked in a saucepan until soft, but not too soft. When meat is done, remove it and add carrot water to liquid in pot; bring to a boil. Thicken with flour-and-water mixture. Return meat and carrots to gravy. Serve over mashed potatoes.

Sunday Dinner

By Rita Akin Sandlin

As far back as I can remember, when I was growing up, we always—and I do mean *always*—had a special dinner on Sunday. We started preparing for Sunday on Saturday, and not just the food. We always washed and rolled our hair, polished our shoes if they needed it, and pressed our dresses. We always took the proverbial Saturday-night bath in the kitchen in a washtub with hot water heated on the gas stove. Mom fixed a pie, cake or Jell-O for dessert for Sunday.

Early Sunday morning, Mom put a roast in the oven at 250 degrees so that it would be done when we got home from church. She peeled her potatoes, cut them up and had them in a pan of water, ready to start cooking them for making mashed potatoes as soon as we got home.

We also had another vegetable—perhaps home-canned green beans, or corn on the cob. In the summer we enjoyed vegetables from Mother's garden, such as English or black-eyed peas, new potatoes, fried okra, boiled carrots or fried squash.

On rare occasions we had a fried chicken from Mother's flock instead of a roast, but I didn't like to have fried chicken because it took too long to cook.

When my sister married and moved away from home, she carried on the Sunday dinner tradition, but she added fresh rolls. She made them before she and her family left for Sunday school. The rolls would rise and be ready to bake by the time they got home and the roast was done.

When I married and left home some 50 years ago, I brought the same tradition to our home. I add carrots to the roast and make roast gravy and cornbread. We always have another vegetable, usually English peas. My granddaughter can't have Sunday dinner without English peas.

I also cook enough food to have some leftovers. I fix homemade TV dinners and freeze them, or make barbecue with the leftover roast.

Following are my recipes for our traditional Sunday dinner. ❖

The recipes on the following page are from An Okie's First Kitchen Cooking Book *by Rita Akin Sandlin, copyright 1984.*

Roast Beef

1 tablespoon grease
3- to 3½-pound boneless chuck roast
½ teaspoon salt
½ teaspoon pepper
½ cup flour
3 cups hot water
3 or 4 carrots, peeled and sliced

Preheat oven to 300 degrees.

Heat grease in roaster pan on top of stove. Salt, pepper and flour both sides of roast. Brown roast on both sides in hot grease, then carefully add hot water to pan.

Move roaster pan to preheated oven and bake for 2½ to 3 hours. You may need to add more hot water in order to have enough drippings for gravy.

When you put the roast in to bake, add 3 or 4 sliced carrots or as many as you like. The roast and carrots will be done at the same time.

Mashed Potatoes

6 medium red potatoes
Boiling water
8 tablespoons butter
3 tablespoons milk
Salt

Peel potatoes and cut into quarters; place in a heavy pot with a good handle and a lid, which are needed when lifting, draining and mashing. Add boiling water to cover and cook for 20 to 30 minutes, until tender. Drain.

Using potato masher, mash through the potatoes in the pot 4 or 5 times. Drop lumps of butter into the hot potatoes and pour in milk; add salt to taste. Keep mashing until the potatoes are smooth, with no lumps. Look for a full, fluffy consistency that is neither runny nor stiff. Taste and add more butter, milk or salt as needed. Makes 6 servings.

Roast Beef Gravy

1½ cups broth from roast beef
½ cup plus 3 tablespoons water, divided
¼ teaspoon salt
3 tablespoons flour

Remove roast beef from oven. Set roaster pan with broth on a burner of stove. Remove roast beef and carrots to serving platter; keep warm. Add ½ cup water and salt to broth in pan. Stir thoroughly. In a small cup, blend flour and remaining 3 tablespoons water, whisking to a smooth consistency with a fork. Stirring constantly, add the mixture to broth in roaster pan and cook over low heat for a few minutes until gravy is thickened and smooth.

1955 General Electric stove ad, House of White Birches nostalgia archives

Thanksgiving Feast

By Erma Todd

About two weeks before Thanksgiving, my Mama started saving eggs, collected from the henhouse, for her cakes and pies. We had a long buffet along one wall in the kitchen. She covered that with a white sheet, and three days before Thanksgiving, she started baking. Cakes and pies started appearing as if by magic.

First came the pecan cake with a little whiskey added for flavor. The pecans were shelled by hand. She used an old flatiron, turned upside-down in her lap, and a tack hammer. Most of the nuts came from their shells unbroken. The best ones she put on the outside of the cake, all over the fluffy, white, seven-minute frosting that stood in peaks. Three-layered raisin cake came next, with frosting and plump raisins between each layer. My favorite cake came next—coconut, moist and yellow inside, with high peaks of frosting and toasted coconut sprinkled all around. All these cakes were made from scratch. I don't think I ever saw a box of cake mix in her kitchen.

Next came the pies—pecan, dark and heavy with pecans, and mincemeat for Dad and me. Everybody else in the house hated mincemeat pie, except us. One more thing to be thankful for! And there was her pumpkin pie that smelled so good, plus coconut pie with egg whites whipped up a mile high and browned ever so lightly on top.

Platters were passed, bowls handed here and there, and glasses filled.

The night before Thanksgiving, Mama made her corn bread for the corn-bread dressing, boiled eggs and potatoes for the potato salad, and chopped celery, cabbage, pickles and onions.

Then the kitchen had to be cleaned and mopped. That was done by my sister and me. We carried water from the barrel outside, heated the water on the stove, washed and dried the dishes, and swept and mopped the floor. We went to bed early because the real work started at about 4:30 a.m. When we got out of bed, we made our beds right away. We did an extra-good job on that day. We lived in a shotgun house, and everybody had to come through our bedroom to get to the kitchen.

Mama would put water on to boil and yell "Come on!" to us. Then we went outside to hunt down that big fat hen and two young fryers she'd had her eye on. The hen was put on to boil for the chicken and dressing, and the fryers were cut up and put in the refrigerator to be fried later. We'd put potatoes on to boil for the mashed potatoes, clean the kitchen again, and take a short break. We ate dinner at noon in Mama's house.

Then she'd come, hair up, apron on, ready to cook. We carried more water for cleanup from the barrels of water we had pumped up outside.

The dressing was made, tearing up last night's corn bread into small pieces, and adding onions and celery that had been fried limp in bacon grease, along with raw eggs, salt, pepper, a big handful of sage, and the broth from the hen. The hen's meat was taken off the bones, mixed with the dressing, and put into the oven.

Potato salad was next. The potatoes were mashed, eggs boiled, onion and celery chopped, and salt, pepper, mayonnaise and a little mustard—for tang—were added. Beans, green and white, were cooked down until the juice was thick and rich. We made fried corn with real butter, milk, salt, pepper and a little bit of sugar, and thickened with cornstarch and cold water.

The frying chicken was breaded with flour, salt and pepper, and then fried a golden brown. Coleslaw was made with shredded cabbage, carrots and a sauce made from eggs, flour, sugar and vinegar that she cooked on top of the stove. Mashed potatoes were made with real butter and milk.

Finally, there were buttermilk biscuits, dripping with real butter, and the "house wine" of the South, iced tea—gallons of it.

Mama never knew how many were coming. Side benches were brought in from the tractor shed and leaves were placed in the table. Then we sat down to eat. Platters were passed, bowls handed here and there, and glasses filled.

Crowded around the table were the people she loved: her children and their children, and some folks we didn't even know, brought home by some of the kids who felt sorry for them because they had no home. They all went home with leftovers every year. I treasure my wonderful memories of a woman who cooked her meals with the best of ingredients, the most important one of which was love. Thank you, Mom. I miss you. ❖

Family Glue

By Kim Kasch

Mom and Dad had nine children when they probably could really afford only two. Still, I didn't realize just how poor we were until much later in life, because Mom was nothing short of amazing.

She could whip up a feast with nothing more than a little pasta and a can of tuna, or create a plethora of pastries to satisfy the hungriest of souls using only a little flour and a can of fruit. Mom used her imagination, especially at holidays, to make meals special. I remember enjoying plentiful but inexpensive meals like Eggs Goldenrod for Easter breakfast and Pinky-Dink Soup for lunch.

While Mom boiled the eggs, we kids were waiting—anxiously—to color them. She would set the broken ones aside for the next morning. Then she'd get up before everyone else to dice the white into a creamy white sauce she'd pour over toast. Then she chopped yolks into a crumbly topping and sprinkled paprika in the center to create a beautiful daffodil to herald the occasion.

But that was just the beginning. Mom raised nine of us and even took my cousins in for a time when her sister was in the hospital. Then, after Granddad died, Mom moved Grandma into the back bedroom and took care of her, too.

Dad didn't make much money working at the mill, and with 12 mouths to feed three times a day, Mom had to be a little crafty with her culinary creations. With vegetables from

the backyard garden, she stretched her meager budget, and when spring had barely sprung, you'd find Mom out in the garden gathering her harvest of beets, lettuce and radishes.

Finally there were too many of us to sit at the table. "Not enough chairs," Dad said, shaking his head; they couldn't afford to buy more.

But Mom always found a way for us to gather around. "Move the chairs out of the kitchen," she told the boys. "Bring the picnic benches in from the back yard." Mom was the family glue that held us together. Even now, when I think back, I still picture Mom sitting at that scratched kitchen table, giving advice when it was asked for. But mostly I remember Mom sitting and listening while others talked—and believe me, they talked and talked for hours, because Mom had a way of making everyone feel welcome to come in and sit at her kitchen table. That's where we ate together. While we told our stories in that shabby kitchen circle, we learned about life and love, and we laughed and cried.

Even now, when we're all grown, we still come back to pull up a seat next to Mom to sit and share around the kitchen table. ❖

Pinky-Dink Soup

2 cups beef broth
3 cups water
1 cup green beans, cut up
1 cup corn
½ cup diced carrots
¼ cup diced onion

1 cup peas
1 cup uncooked macaroni
½ cup sliced celery
½ cup beets

Combine all ingredients in a big soup pot and bring to a boil over high heat. Reduce the heat and simmer for 1½ hours, stirring occasionally. The soup becomes a thick stew when done, and the pink color helps herald spring.

A Mysterious Sandwich

By Edna Krause

Lunchtime was always the most pleasant and interesting part of the day at our upper Michigan school. Not only did it still our growling stomachs, but also it was a time for lively conversation.

One day Muriel acted very secretive about her new kind of sandwich. We were anxious to know why her sandwich looked so scrumptious, but we were too polite to ask. It looked like the filling was made with peanuts. And how we all craved peanuts!

As I ate my jelly sandwich, I saw that Margaret had a peanut butter sandwich, Josephine munched on a mayonnaise sandwich and, of course, Stella had her standby that permeated the air with a strong, oniony smell. "My mother fried an onion in lard," she told us, "and after it set, I made sandwiches with it."

We sat around the table, laughing and talking, while our lunch pails and the brown paper in which our sandwiches had been wrapped lay scattered before us.

There was Stella's lard pail with "White Star Pure Lard" printed on it in bold letters, and Margaret's brown and yellow peanut butter pail. Seldom did anyone bring a drink in the lunch bucket. We drank from a portable water fountain in the room. We felt fortunate that we didn't have to go outside to the pump.

Around 1948, the principal announced a new plan: High school girls would make soup every day in school. My dad donated vegetables and Margaret's mother supplied the home-canned tomatoes. The other parents took turns bringing nourishing produce to school. Sometimes the local store donated a soup bone to flavor the tasty vegetable soup.

Each student brought a bowl with his or her name taped to the bottom. By the time the labels fell off, we all recognized our own bowls. (I still have the bowl I used in high school.)

With the 5-cent bowl of good, hot soup, I ate my jelly sandwich. I noticed that Muriel still brought her mysterious sandwich, and was just as secretive about it.

One day when Muriel was absent, her sandwich was the topic of discussion. We all wondered how she possibly could afford a peanut sandwich; the rest of us enjoyed peanuts only at Christmastime.

"Why were you all always staring at my sandwich?" Muriel asked.

Eventually the money collected for the soup accumulated and the school began to offer 5-cent hot dogs every Thursday. My friends and I danced with joy when we heard the good news. A hot dog looked even more delicious than Muriel's sandwich!

I saved my pennies, but still couldn't buy a hot dog every week. Sometimes my older sister surprised me with one when she knew that I had no money. But many students couldn't afford hot dogs every week, so I didn't feel left out. Now, with our minds focused on hot dogs, we showed little interest in Muriel's mysterious sandwich. She, in turn, became more relaxed at lunch.

Then one day Muriel asked, "Why were you all always staring at my sandwich? I thought you were making fun of it, and I felt embarrassed."

"No, no!" I shot back. "Your sandwich looked so good, like it was filled with peanuts—and we all yearn for peanuts. You might say we ate your sandwich with our eyes."

"Well," Muriel said, smiling, "it's not peanuts. It's beans."

We looked at each other and burst out laughing. All of us ate plenty of beans at home, but it never crossed our minds to use beans in a sandwich! The longed-for sandwich lost its glamour, and we giggled with embarrassment to think how we yearned for something we already had. ❖

Table Setting – Dinner No. 2.

Soup
   Meat Loaf (1)
   Corn Pudding (2)
   Stewed Tomatoes (3)
   Sweet Rolls (4)
Pineapple Upside Down
     Cake

Cunningham Café

By Ethel Weehunt

Elsie Cunningham was the new home-economics teacher at Okemah High School in the fall of 1926. My sister, Ruth, and I enrolled in her cooking class. We had to wear an apron-style smock that covered our clothes, and we had to have an oak recipe box. Our teacher called the class to order in the basement of the junior-high building, where somehow she had managed to have five tabletop gas stoves installed and one large range. In an adjoining room, three long tables with benches had been installed. We sat at the tables.

Introductions were made all around. Then Miss Cunningham, in her brisk, friendly voice, said, "Girls, I welcome you to a class where you are going to learn by experience how to cook nutritious food, which you are going to *sell*. I have received permission from the officials to install a café! We will cook and serve meals." She paused and looked around the room at the surprised faces.

"Now," she asked, "does anyone have a name for this innovative idea?"

> *"You are going to learn by experience how to cook nutritious food."*

"Yes," Ruth bravely answered. "How about The Cunningham Café?" Miss Cunningham bowed her head modestly as the class clapped. "Yes, yes!" they heartily agreed.

And so the café began. It was advertised in the school paper. Our menu included beef stew for 25 cents, a "plate lunch" with two vegetables and meat loaf or another meat entrée for 40 cents, and chocolate, cherry and lemon meringue pies for 20 cents a wedge.

Serving this menu on a daily basis required all-out preparation by each of the two morning classes—14 girls, working steadily at their assigned tasks. But Miss Cunningham was not only creative, she was an organizer. She knew how to balance food preparation and time.

That first day, the faculty flocked in. We ran out of food, and had to turn away would-be diners. The tables and benches were full.

As the days passed, we gradually were able to better synchronize our food and our customers. And we made a profit. When the noon meal was over, our wonderful teacher would sack up the money and send two girls to the bank, where Miss Cunningham had opened an account for The Cunningham Café.

Occasionally the café would serve hot dinner rolls. This meant that someone had to be in the kitchen by 8 a.m. to start the rolls. We divided the class into pairs, with every couple taking a turn at the early duty. We lived three miles from school, so Ruth and I had to rise early for a walk through the fresh morning air when it was our turn to start the rolls.

News of Elsie Cunningham's creative enterprise spread. Eventually she left us for a better-paying job, organizing cafés in other schools.

Of all the many teachers I had during the Good Old Days, back when teachers were allowed to use their own abilities, none taught me more about using one's own God-given talents than Miss Cunningham. ❖

These recipes are for two of the most popular items served at the Cunningham Café.

Cherry Pie

I think the most difficult thing about Miss Cunningham's cooking class was learning the art of making crispy piecrust.

Filling: ½ cup flour
          ½ cup sugar
          1 small can cherries
          1 tablespoon butter

Crust: 1½ cups flour
          1 teaspoon salt
          ½ teaspoon baking powder
          ½ cup fat, chilled
          ½ cup water

For piecrust, sift together flour, salt and baking powder. Cut in cold fat with knife and fork until a mealy texture is achieved. Mix in water a little at a time, adding just enough to make a dough. Divide dough in half; roll out in circles to make top and bottom crusts. Cut top crust in strips for lattice top, if desired.

For filling, combine flour and sugar; add to cherries and cook until slightly thickened. Add butter. Pour mixture into pan lined with unbaked piecrust. Cover with top crust or lattice crust. Bake in moderate oven until crust is brown.

Potatoes on the Half Shell

Select smooth, medium-sized potatoes. Wash well with a small vegetable brush. Dry. Coat potatoes with a thin layer of grease and prick with a fork several times. Bake in a hot oven for about 45 minutes, or until done. Cut the end from each baked potato or cut in half lengthwise. Scrape out the insides with a fork; mash, then season with salt, pepper, butter and milk. Fill the skins with the mixture, but do not pack. Brush tops with well-beaten egg white, sprinkle with grated cheese, and return to oven until brown. Minced meat may be added to the potato, if desired.

Chomp

By Anna Witman

When iron-producing furnaces were popping up all over Pennsylvania like an epidemic of measles, the wives of the workers carried lunch to their husbands so that the men would not waste important time walking home to eat.

No matter what the menu, a raw salad was appreciated. Molders and furnace fillers had no way of protecting themselves from the charcoal dust, smoke and gases that filled the air, so they were constantly thirsty. Water boys brought water often, but it was not enough, and the raw vegetable salad with vinegar dressing was very refreshing.

From the first wild greens of early spring until the last bit of endive in late fall, every salad was made with a simple vinegar dressing. Try it. You'll like it. Experiment and add the vegetables you prefer. No one knows how we got the name "Chomp," unless it sounded like *chomp-chomp* when eaten. The recipe has been with us for more than 150 years. ❖

Chomp

2 large sliced cucumbers
1 large green pepper, diced
1 large onion, diced
2 firm, ripe tomatoes, cut in wedges
½ cup brown sugar
½ cup water
½ cup vinegar
1 teaspoon salt
½ teaspoon black pepper
⅛ teaspoon powdered thyme

Combine fresh vegetables. Mix remaining ingredients for dressing; blend well. Mix dressing with vegetables and chill for 1 hour before serving.

Grandma's Soup

By Renie Szilak Burghardt

Paprikash soup was the favorite soup of my childhood in Hungary. My grandmother, who raised me, cooked it often for Grandpa and me and called it *krumpli leves*, which translates into "potato soup."

Years later I renamed it, and I felt the new name was most appropriate. In any case, it was always delicious, and it was always there—a sort of security soup.

When we escaped from Russian-occupied Hungary in the late 1940s, we ended up in a displaced persons camp in Austria. There, along with hundreds of other DPs of various nationalities, we lived in old army barracks and went to the common kitchen with our tin-can "bowls." The usual fare served to us in camp was watery cabbage soup, along with a hunk of black bread and a pat of margarine. We children also rated a daily ration of milk.

How Grandpa and I missed Grandma's soup! We reminisced about it longingly, our mouths watering. But during the four years we spent in that camp, there was no cooking to be done for Grandma, and no good eating to be had for us. The times, of course, were hard, and we were lucky to be alive, so it didn't matter that I hated that watery cabbage; it nevertheless kept me nourished.

When in the early 1950s we were fortunate enough to immigrate to America to start a new life, my grandparents found jobs while I went to school. It was then that Grandma taught me to make paprikash soup. I was 13 and the first one home every day, so she felt I was old enough to start supper. She didn't exactly have a recipe. She just chopped an onion here, some carrots and potatoes there, and threw in some paprika and whatever else was available. Still, it always turned out delicious.

After watching her, I followed suit, expecting the worst—but it turned out as good as Grandma's! Well, at least that's what Grandpa told me, when he came home from work to his favorite soup. We ate paprikash soup often during the first couple of years because it was economical, and my grandparents were saving for a home. They were able to realize this dream within two years, thanks partially to paprikash soup, but mainly to our wonderful new country, where such things were possible.

I have personalized the original recipe by adding other vegetables and rice or noodles, but the soup is still quick, delicious, nutritious and beautiful, as well. *Jó Étvágyat!* (Good appetite!) ❖

Paprikash Soup, Hungarian Style

1 large onion, chopped
2 tablespoons oil or margarine
4 carrots, cut up
4 large potatoes, cut up
8 cups water
10 ounces frozen corn
¼ cup half-and-half or milk

2 tablespoons paprika
4 stalks celery, chopped
¼ cup rice, brown or white
Salt and pepper to taste
10 ounces frozen peas

Sauté onion in oil until tender. Add paprika; stir. Add next 4 ingredients; cook for 5 minutes to blend flavors. Add water, salt and pepper. Bring to a simmer and cook for about 40 minutes. Ten minutes before done, add frozen vegetables. Stir in half-and-half, heat up and enjoy. Makes 6 servings.

Radio Recipes

By Dorothy Rieke

Even today, long after the last radio-homemaker broadcast, I miss those special ladies who were featured for 30 minutes each day on our local radio station. During their "visits," those personalities, so well versed in cooking, baking and cleaning, gave favorite recipes, interesting food ideas and household hints, as well as advice and counsel. In short, they helped others learn better food preparation, promoted the fun of eating, and offered friendship and company for stay-at-home housewives.

Each weekday morning, if I was not especially busy, I tuned in to radio station KMA in Shenandoah, Iowa, to hear conversation and recipes from those on the broadcast. Several other stations, including KFNF and KOTD, occasionally featured homemakers, too, but KMA became the "star performer" of homemaker shows through the years.

Listeners not only acquired new recipes and useful household hints, but they often aspired to meet that radio personality. During the early years, coffee and tea were served by the reigning homemaker at the station. However, this project grew too large to handle. Later, in the 1950s, a cookie tea was instituted, but that, too, was discontinued after a few years.

Some of the homemakers I remember on KMA were Bernice Currier, the Driftmier sisters, Billie Oakley, Brenda Kay McConnaughey, Verlene Luker, Florence Falk and Evelyn Birkby.

An ongoing recipe exchange developed during those broadcasts. I copied numerous recipes in loose-leaf notebooks, always intending to improve my cooking skills and impress my husband. The radio homemaker gleaned recipes from her kitchen experience, but listeners also contributed. We had confidence in those recipes shared over the airwaves, as most had been tested by the radio personality. No one wanted to waste flour, sugar and other ingredients on something the family would not eat.

The Driftmier family—mother Leanna, Margie, Lucille and Dorothy—took turns at the microphone for their weekday show, *Kitchen Klatter*. The family supplemented their radio visits with an intriguing little magazine, also called *Kitchen Klatter*. It offered articles by family members telling about their work, families and activities.

A few articles were written by outsiders, such as Mabel Nair Brown, who submitted monthly pieces giving suggestions for club and church programs and parties.

The Driftmier family, so innovative in numerous ways, published a 463-page cookbook in 1973 that contained recipes featured on

their radio program along with other favorites. Undoubtedly these recipes represented many happy hours spent in food preparation.

To this day, this cookbook remains a good reference if one is searching for a particular dependable recipe.

Later, as they discovered more terrific recipes, the family published several smaller specialty cookbooks, including *The Best of Kitchen Klatter Dessert Recipes.*

This group also produced commercial products such as salad dressings, sweeteners, a variety of flavorings, and cleaners.

In fact, their flavorings included raspberry, orange, maple, cherry, burnt sugar, black walnut, almond, butterscotch, coconut, butter, blueberry, banana, peach, strawberry, pineapple, mint, lemon, chocolate, cinnamon and two kinds of vanilla.

Of course, many recipes given on their radio program called for their flavorings and salad dressings, and helped increase Driftmier Co. sales.

The Driftmiers often traveled to radio-broadcast locations to promote their products. These visits helped increase the number of listeners, product sales and magazine subscriptions.

In fact, their popularity was such that bus tours and carloads of visitors came to Shenandoah to visit the Kitchen Klatter plant, and Margie's and Leanna's gardens, and catch a glimpse of those famous radio personalities. Much of this family's acceptance rested on their creative cooking abilities and their friendliness.

Another homemaker featured years ago on the radio was Bernice Currier. She was a musician-turned-radio-homemaker. Undoubtedly she was a good cook because her show featured some very good recipes.

CHERRY JELL-O CORONET

1 package Cherry Jell-O
1 pint hot water
¾ cup seeded canned white cherries
1½ cups fresh grapefruit sections, free from membrane

Dissolve Jell-O in hot water. Arrange cherries in bottom of mold. Pour on Jell-O, being careful not to disarrange cherries. Add grapefruit. Chill until firm. Unmold. Garnish with grapefruit sections and green leaves. For large mold, double recipe but decrease hot water to 3½ cups. (*All measurements are level.*)

Meet us on the air Sunday Night!

Tune in Sunday night for the gayest, grandest show on the air! Laugh with Jack Benny, America's most popular comedian, and his lively partner, Mary Livingstone. Don Wilson announcing, Kenny Baker singing, Phil Harris' orchestra. 7 P.M. Eastern Standard Time, 6 Central, 9:30 Mountain, 8:30 Pacific. N.B.C. Network. It's "Jell-O again!"

A product of General Foods.

Strawberry • Raspberry • Cherry • Orange • Lemon • Lime

Her recipes were often organized in an easy-to-understand form, using the alphabet. "A" group represented dry ingredients, "B" represented liquid ingredients, and so on. Directions for preparation were easy with this arrangement.

Another of my favorite homemakers on KMA was a lighthearted, excellent cook, Billie Oakley. Her personality enlivened her show, making everyone feel better.

Cooking for her three children and her social contacts more than qualified her for creating and sharing excellent recipes with her radio audience. Billie was a creative cook with an instinctive taste for good food.

When she opened her radio show to listeners' recipes and comments, she gleaned enough recipes from call-ins to publish *Billie Oakley's Everybody's an Expert Cookbook.*

Later she published *Billie Oakley's Golden Memories*, a cookbook tribute to the pioneer women who "made do" with available ingredients and utensils to give families the comforts of home.

Many chapters are prefaced with a short memory piece, including "The One-Room Country Schoolhouse," "Outhouse Memories," "Bless the Feed Sacks" and others.

This lady was also responsible for publishing *Home Talk*, a magazine similar to the Driftmier publication, which featured recipes and helpful articles. The pithy, humorous sayings delighted readers.

Radio personalities advertised to pay for radio time. Of course, many listeners took radio personalities' words as "gold," so when Billie Oakley began advertising Bag Balm and talked about how she used the salve, the demand for Bag Balm increased. In fact, one drugstore ordered and reordered Bag Balm in large and small tins for quite some time.

Perhaps the "crowning glory" of all these radio broadcasts was the exciting, popular Cookie Festival, revived in 1978 to be held annually. Attendance began at 600 that first year and grew to almost 1,000 in 1982. The "admission fee" was one dozen cookies plus the recipe.

Festival events were planned, including demonstrations by home economists and contests with prizes for the best cookies in each division. One event was the "Cookie Walk," which included viewing cookies brought by participants. The cookies were variations of older recipes as well as brand-new recipes, resulting in a variety of types and styles.

Later, guests sampled the cookies. Those left were given to senior citizen centers and a children's home. Several very funny encounters at festivals left homemakers laughing. One gentleman brought "Castor Oil Cookies" and insisted that his favorite cookies were "surprisingly good."Another time, when the event was held in the early fall, the heat was so bad that the cookies—and participants—nearly melted!

Another year, such a crowd appeared that some ladies, holding their plates of cookies, were left standing outside the building.

These festivals gave listeners an opportunity to demonstrate their baking talents, meet radio personalities, attend "learning" demonstrations, make new friends and renew old acquaintances. They were special times shared by those who were bonded together by radio homemakers.

One commercial outcome of these gatherings was the publication of two cookie recipe books, *Festival Cookie Book* and *Come Again Cookie Book*, both compiled by Evelyn Birkby.

I truly enjoyed homemaker radio programs. As a beginning homemaker, I learned much from those broadcasts. In fact, I continue to use those hastily written recipes in seven notebooks. Listening to those women telling their experiences was like conversing with friends.

I sympathized with them in their troubles and gloried in their achievements. Those shows—and the recipes that follow on the next page—represent sweet memories for me. ❖

JACK BENNY and the DUKE

JACK: You were so kind last summer in France, André —we do hope you'll get a big kick out of America!
MARY: Yes, indeed! Aren't you thrilled at the New York sky line?
THE DUKE: H'm. It is not so high as I expect.

MARY: Ah—what majesty in the thunder of those waters! Jack—I've written a poem—
JACK: Hush, Mary. But isn't it awe-inspiring, André?
THE DUKE: Me—I am reminded. Did I turn off the faucette in the bathroom?

JACK: Think of it, André—these redwood trees were old when Columbus discovered America!
MARY: This one's 340 feet high and 28 feet thick!
THE DUKE: Um-hm. For my chateau, they would make the nice hedge.

THE DUKE: So bad a crack—you would think they would fix it.
MARY: Where'll we take him for dinner?
JACK: Oh, I give up trying to impress this guy. Let's go to Molly's Cafe—I like her cooking.

THE DUKE: Mademoiselle Mol-lee make these dessert so marvelous? I shall make her the offer of marriage.
JACK: But André—I thought you wanted an heiress.
THE DUKE: What is gold?...I have find the woman who make the most glorious dessert in the universe! ¶

MARY: But listen, André—wait a minute. *Anybody* can make this dish! That is, any one who uses real extra-rich Jell-O and not some flat-tasting imitation. Why, *every American woman can make a dessert just like this!*
THE DUKE: Mon dieu!...What a countree!

Dessert Salad
This Driftmier recipe was given over the radio.

¼ cup vinegar
¼ cup sugar
2 eggs, beaten
¼ teaspoon each cherry, pineapple
    and orange flavorings
2 tablespoons butter or margarine
1 cup cream
2 cups white cherries, pitted,
    or green grapes
2 cups diced pineapple
2 oranges, peeled and diced
2 cup miniature marshmallows

Cook vinegar, sugar, eggs and flavorings in a double boiler until thick; remove from heat. Add butter; stir until melted. Let cool. Whip cream; fold into cooked mixture. Add fruits and marshmallows. Refrigerate for 24 hours before serving.

Applesauce Fruitcake
This is one of Billie Oakley's recipes from my notebooks. Add more fruit and nuts, if desired. In this case, the more the better.

1 cup shortening or 2 sticks margarine
2 cups sugar
2½ cups hot applesauce
2 large eggs, beaten
4 cups flour
4 teaspoons baking soda
1 teaspoon salt
1 teaspoon cinnamon
½ teaspoon ground cloves
2 cups white raisins
1 cup slivered almonds
2 cups candied fruit—a mixture
    of pineapple and red cherries

Preheat oven to 350 degrees. Grease a 9 x 13-inch baking pan well.

Cream shortening and sugar. Blend in applesauce and eggs; stir mixture well.

Sift together flour, baking soda, salt, cinnamon and cloves three times. Add dry ingredients to applesauce mixture and beat well. Fold in the raisins, nuts and candied fruit; stir again.

Bake prepared baking pan for 55 minutes, or until done when tested with a cake tester. This can be cut into 6 small loaves, and it freezes well. Wrap and freeze for gifts.

Brenda Kay's Asparagus Salad

1 (8-ounce) package cream cheese
    at room temperature
1 cup or 1 small can asparagus soup
2 (3-ounce) packages lime gelatin
1 cup boiling water
1 cup mayonnaise or salad dressing
½ cup chopped pecans
1 cup chopped green pepper
    (or less to taste)
1½ cups chopped celery

Oil a gelatin mold. Add cream cheese to asparagus soup; beat until creamy. Dissolve gelatin in boiling water. Let cool. Combine with other ingredients. Pour into oiled mold. Refrigerate until firm.

Mock Chow Mein
Florence Falk gave this recipe over the radio. This can be frozen and baked later.

1½ pounds ground beef
1 cup diced celery
1 to 2 cups cooked rice
1 can cream of mushroom soup
1 can cream of chicken soup
2 soup cans water
2 tablespoons soy sauce
Chow mein noodles

Preheat oven to 350 degrees. Combine all ingredients except chow mein noodles. Pour into large baking pan.

Top with chow mein noodles. Bake for 30 to 45 minutes.

Patriotism Isn't Corny

By Anna Witman

During World War I, I was very small, but I remember celebrating the Fourth of July. This particular year, fireworks were scarce and expensive, and my two older brothers lamented the fact that we would not have a happy holiday.

Mother gave us a pep talk about patriotism and how necessary it was to save gunpowder. (I think, however, that it really was money she was trying to save.)

She promised to cook supper outdoors if the boys would make homemade fireworks, so they manufactured things *resembling* fireworks from dried grass, bark, pinecones and tall stalks of dried weeds.

We ate in the orchard, seated on the ground around a flat stone that was easily 10 feet in diameter. Supper consisted of flapjacks done over the open fire, corn chowder, cherry pie and Grammy's famous lemonade.

I can still see Grandfather with his snow-white hair and mustache, and I can still see Grammy's sweet face. ❖

Corn Chowder
Best when fresh corn is used.

4 diced potatoes
1 cup diced celery
1 cup diced onions
1 cup diced carrots
1 cup diced green pepper
Salt
Water
1 cup fresh sweet corn kernels
2 cups fresh milk
2 tablespoons butter
1 tablespoon sugar
1 tablespoon fresh parsley
Hard-cooked egg (optional)

Cook potatoes, celery, onions, carrots and green pepper in slightly salted water until tender. Add sweet corn kernels; boil for 5 minutes.

Pour off most of the water. Add milk, butter, sugar and parsley. Bring to a simmer but do not boil. Taste for seasoning; serve hot. Add sliced hard-cooked egg, if desired.

Chicken Love Story

By J.B. Cearley

*S*unday dinner. My older brother and I were starving as we hoofed it home that hot August day from our country church in West Texas. The 3½-mile walk got us home at about 1 o'clock. As I stepped onto the long wooden porch and approached the kitchen, I smelled fried chicken. I was famished. Chicken was our main source of meat during the Depression of the 1930s. Electricity was unheard of in rural Texas. Keeping meat was almost impossible in the 100-degree heat, so we frequently had chicken that we raised on the farm. We often had meatless meals.

I hurried into the kitchen as Mother finished setting the food on the table. She had baked hot biscuits in the oven of her old kerosene stove. There was a pot of pinto beans, a bowl of corn, and a platter of fried potatoes.

The old stove had only three burners for cooking, and Mother used them wisely, giving us the best diet possible for poor farmers during the Dust Bowl days on the high plains.

Then I asked, "Why can't I have the back and gizzard sometime?"

I hurried to wash and dropped into my chair beside my older brother. Mother took her place, and then we had the blessing. I watched as Mother took the plate of fried chicken and forked out the pulley bone and gave it to my little sister, age 5. She was sitting on the bench by our younger brother, who was 8. Mother passed the chicken around the table.

I watched as Dad took the gizzard, neck and a thigh. Little brother got one of the breasts, and my older brother got the other. Mother took the back and the liver.

When my turn arrived, I took a thigh. Then I helped myself to beans, creamed corn and potatoes. I buttered biscuits and began to satisfy my hunger with the tasty food.

My thoughts drifted back to the time when I got the pulley bone, that rare piece of chicken that is so easy to eat and has such delicious white meat. Mother knew that the smallest child deserved that delicacy. When a new child was old enough to sit and eat at the table, she gave that youngster the pulley bone.

She had a special way of carving a chicken so that there were many good pieces. Store-bought chicken does not have a pulley bone.

As we ate, I began to wonder why Mother and Dad always got their special pieces of chicken. I puzzled over this for a few minutes. Then I asked, "Why can't I have the back and gizzard sometime?"

Mother and Dad looked at me in surprise. Then mother asked, "You really want the back?"

Facing page: *First Chicken Dinner*, House of White Birches nostalgia archives

"Yes, I'd like to try it," I said.

"The next time we have chicken, you can have the back and the gizzard," she said, smiling at Dad.

On Tuesday we again had chicken for the noon meal. (Oatmeal or eggs and bread was the kids' breakfast, and we usually had meatless suppers.)

When we were seated at the table that noon, I watched as Mother again gave Little Sister the pulley bone. Then she passed the plate to me. I quickly took the back and gizzard for my big feast!

Did I ever get a surprise. There wasn't enough meat on that back to feed a flea! I got no meat at all from it. And that gizzard proved to be tough chewing, and I didn't like its taste. Why, then, did the folks always take those pieces like they were delicacies?

It was then that I realized that they ate the skimpy pieces so that their growing children could have some good meat. The breasts, pulley bone, thighs and legs had the good meat.

I realized that day that my parents truly loved their children. They were sacrificing all they could for our health. That day, I was in awe of my parents.

After that day, I never fussed about what part of the chicken I had to eat. I was happy with a leg, thigh or anything with a little meat.

I then understood about love. Our pastor had preached a sermon about Jesus feeding 5,000 men besides women and children after a lad had given the disciples his lunch of five barley loaves and two small fish. Why should he give up his lunch when he was hungry? I then understood that he had given his lunch out of love for others, just as Jesus had done so many times (John 6: 9–13).

After this, I appreciated my parents. I knew that they were sacrificing for me out of their love. ❖

Old-Fashioned Bean Soup, Modernized

By Aline Ellen

When I married, I felt confident I could handle all the ups and downs, but doubted I could please my husband with my cooking. I was convinced I could never match his mother's fabulous cooking. She came to America from the German-Austrian-Hungarian-Czechoslovakian border, so he was brought up on European cooking.

Determined to have a contented husband, I asked his mother to teach me how to cook his favorite dishes. She was happy to do so, but when it came time to jot down recipes, I ran into trouble.

She couldn't tell me exact quantities; she "sprinkled" some of this and that, and measured ingredients such as flour, sugar and lard in handfuls or cups. She knew by touch when the dough was right for noodles, bread or pastry. So although I wrote down the recipes,

I was on my own, always experimenting with the quantities.

Eventually, by trial and error, I got it right, and several of her recipes became favorites of my family. Now that I'm a widowed grandma living alone, I still make large batches of special recipes, but I freeze them in individual servings. My children keep me in practice, for they call upon me to make big pots of chili, spaghetti sauce, noodle soup, sour-cream dumplings/potato dish, and bean soup to freeze for their families.

This past Christmas, ham was the meat of choice. One son who ate Christmas Eve dinner at a friend's house came to my house afterward with the biggest ham bone I have ever seen. His friend had served a whole, fresh ham and had given him leftover meat and bones, which he gave to me. We had ham again the next day at my daughter's home, where we all gathered to celebrate Christmas Day, and she also gave me leftovers. And I already had bought half a small ham to make bean soup for myself to freeze.

I decided to combine my ham with the leftovers I had been given and invite the family for a casual bean-soup dinner. Since I needed enough soup to feed almost a dozen people, I doubled the original recipe. I was forced to cook the soup in a canner; none of my soup kettles was large enough.

My family arrived with tongues hanging out. They dished out their own bowls of soup, buttered thick slices of fresh Italian bread, and took turns sitting at the kitchen table to eat. When one drooling son arrived, he made a beeline for the kitchen and stopped dead in his tracks at the sight of the huge canner on the stove. Lifting the lid to take a whiff, he yelled to his other half, "Come here and check this out!"

I served this bean soup as a one-dish meal, but my mother-in-law served hers differently. She removed the cooked beans from the broth, added homemade cooked noodles, and served that first, followed by the beans, sliced ham and a salad. Sometimes she put the beans through a sieve and added sour cream to the broth. ❖

Old-Fashioned Bean Soup, Modernized

1 small package navy or Great Northern beans
½ small ham with bone in
1 package celery hearts, chopped
1 large onion, chopped
Water
Chicken bouillon cubes (optional)
1 large package Pennsylvania Dutch medium noodles
Salt to taste

Wash beans, removing any debris or bad beans. Cover beans with cold water and let soak overnight. Drain beans; put in pot with ham, bone, chopped celery and onion. Cover with water. Heat to boiling. Reduce heat; cover tightly and simmer until beans are soft, 2 to 3 hours.

During cooking, check to see if water is low and add more water or chicken bouillon cubes dissolved in boiling water. If you wish to put beans through a sieve, cook them until mushy.

If you used a cooked ham, remove it before beans are done. Cooked hams do not require lengthy cooking. After ham has cooled, cut meat in small pieces and add to broth.

Cook noodles separately; rinse well and add to broth.

Some hams are salty; add salt only when soup is done, or when you have sampled the broth for flavor after removing the ham.

Pressure-cooker method: First cook ham, celery and onion together for 25 to 30 minutes. Remove ham; when cool, cut into small pieces. Cook beans (which have soaked overnight) in the broth for 40 minutes. Cool cooker at once.

Cook noodles separately; rinse well and add to broth along with ham. If broth is too thick, add chicken bouillon dissolved in boiling water. Plain water may be added if broth has sufficient flavor. Add salt if needed.

The Root Beer Blew!

By Mary J. Kellar

We had few treats growing up during the 1930s–1950s, but one thing we did look forward to was the rare occasion when Mom made root beer. It was a job that required patience and hard work. First she had to save some money from the meager household budget to buy the ingredients and the new, shiny, gold bottle caps. Then we four children all had to complete a job that was both fun and troublesome: We had to go along the road and collect all the pop bottles that people threw out.

I was both happy and apprehensive about this task. But armed with a gunnysack and my old, faithful bike—named "Champion" after my idol Gene Autry's horse—I was ready to take it on. My three siblings and I looked along separate roads. We loved Pepsi and Dr. Pepper bottles best because they were bigger, but necessity dictated that we gather *all* soda bottles, large and small.

I knew one or two spots where people parked and threw out several bottles at a time. Soon my road was finished and I started the five-mile trek home. My gunnysack, tied securely at the top, was flung over my shoulder. I was sweaty and dirty when I reached home.

Root-beer caps were flying off like small golden saucers!

After we'd unloaded all the bottles and put the gunnysacks away in the shed, we were always told, "You kids go wash your hands. God only knows what germs are on those bottles or who's drank out of them!" That should have dampened our excitement for root beer, but it never did.

Mom washed and bleached all the bottles herself, not trusting the job to anyone else. She wanted those bottles clean! Then we rinsed them and put them in a large copper boiler and set them to sterilizing.

Then she started the root beer. Into a very large kettle she poured sugar, root-beer extract, yeast and water, adding all the ingredients a little at a time. When she boiled it, the whole house smelled of root beer. How anxious we were to taste it, but it would be several days more before we could do anything but smell the tantalizing brew.

My older brother was called in to help Mom with the capping. I wiped each freshly capped bottle with a damp cloth, and my older sister put the bottles on the shelf.

Mom said the root beer had to "work," or "ripen," as some would say. We had no choice but to wait until it was ready. However, my waiting had just about petered out that year, and when I saw a little left in the boiling dish, I quickly drank it without telling anyone.

Suddenly, the root beer began to work on me. I ran to the bathroom, where I was very sick for what seemed like forever. Almost equally agonizing was enduring Mom's haven't-I-always-told-you-never-to-drink-warm-root-beer lecture.

I was so sick that I never did it again.

That year, to add to the complication of waiting, I could not watch the root beer as it worked. Usually Mom put it out in a cool spot in the workshop, but Dad had extra buckets of paint and was mixing colors on the counter.

So Mom said that she would have to put it under the kitchen cupboards that year. "It's warmer, but it will just work faster," she said as my sister added the last bottle. That news delighted us. We could hardly wait for the treat!

1922 Charles E. Hires Co. Rootbeer ad,
House of White Birches nostalgia archives

On a hot summer day, three days before the root beer should have been ready to drink, we were all eating dinner inside because of the excessive heat.

Mom had just fixed us sandwiches and given each of us a glass of Kool-Aid when an awful popping resounded through the whole house. Mom ran to the porch and peered outside. We children were frightened. It sounded like someone was shooting a gun.

Suddenly a huge brown stream started running across the kitchen floor. Mom ran to open the cupboard. Root-beer caps were flying off like small golden saucers, and root beer gushed from the bottlenecks like lava from exploding volcanoes.

Mom roared with relief and laughter, but I failed to see the humor in the situation. My small blue eyes grew wide with horror as my long-dreamed-of root beer continued to run across the floor and puddle at my feet.

I didn't see anything funny at all. In fact, as my siblings hurried to help Mom mop up the mess, small, silent tears dripped down my face. My delicious root beer was no more. I knew I would have to wait a long, long time before Mom could save enough money to buy more ingredients.

Insult was added to injury when I bemoaned the 2-cents-apiece deposit I could have had if I had turned in the bottles.

Many years have passed since the day the root beer exploded. Now, in hindsight, I laugh as my mother did then. We lost our root beer that day, but we gained memories that would be shared as we told and retold the story, handed down from generation to generation.

That story of the day the root beer blew has given more joy and laughter than any root beer ever could.

I have had many kinds of root beer since that long-ago summer day, but none has ever had the robust flavor like the kind we made at home when we were kids. ❖

The root-beer recipe below is reprinted from a 1912 booklet published by the Fleischman Co.

Root Beer

1 cake compressed yeast
5 pounds sugar
2 ounces sassafras root
2 ounces juniper berries
1 ounce dandelion root
1 ounce hops or gingerroot
4 gallons water
2 ounces wintergreen

Wash roots well in cold water. Add juniper berries (crushed) and hops. Pour 8 quarts boiling water over root mixture and boil slowly 20 minutes. Strain through flannel bag. Add sugar and remaining 8 quarts water. Allow to stand until lukewarm.

Dissolve yeast in a little cool water. Add to root liquid. Stir well. Let settle, then strain again and bottle. Cork tightly. Keep in a warm room 5 or 6 hours, then store in a cool place. Pour over ice as required for use.

Dressing & Pressing Chicken

By Frances Grimes Yeargin

As I look through my grandmother's handwritten cookbook, I am amazed that cooks of her day were as successful as tradition has it. Few of her recipes give accurate measurements, sizes of bowls, types of pans, oven temperatures, or length of time for cooking. Here is how Grandmother recorded her recipe for Pressed Chicken.

As I recall, it was considered a special treat and was served to dinner guests or at ladies' luncheons. Grandmother didn't say how many people could be served, but I know that the meat from two hens will feed a crowd.

Grandmother's Pressed Chicken

2 large hens
8 hard-boiled eggs
1 bottle of Lee & Perrin
    Worcester sauce (sic)
1 tablespoon of Tabasco sauce
½ dozen sour pickles
1 box Knox acidulated gelatin
    dissolved in 1½ cups of cold
    water, then poured into a quart of
    rich chicken broth
Salt and pepper to taste

Pour into molds and chill for 24 hours.

That is the complete recipe; there is not a word about what to do with those hens.

As late as 1935–1940, most country girls knew how to dress and cut up a chicken for frying. Cut-up chicken wrapped in plastic was not available in grocery stores until years later.

Grandmother did not give advice about how to boil those large hens. I suppose she assumed that anyone who planned to make Pressed Chicken would know these preliminary preparations. I have changed Grandmother's recipe to include just one chicken. If she were living today, I think Grandmother would press chicken this way:

1925 Indian Head Permanent Finish ad,
House of White Birches nostalgia archives

Pressed Chicken

4½- to 5-pound chicken,
    whole or cut up
1 quart hot water
1 rib celery
1 slice onion
1 sprig parsley
1 carrot
1 tablespoon salt, or less to taste
2 tablespoons unflavored gelatin
2 tablespoons cold water
2 tablespoons Worcestershire sauce
1 tablespoon Tabasco sauce
3 sour pickles, chopped
4 hard-cooked eggs, chopped

Place chicken in 4½-quart kettle with hot water, celery, onion, parsley, carrot and salt. Cover and simmer for 1½ to 2½ hours or until very tender. Let chicken cool in liquid. When the chicken is cool enough to handle, remove from broth and cut into small pieces. Discard bones and skin.

Measure 1 quart of stock from cooking pot. Add gelatin dissolved in cold water. Stir in chicken, Worcestershire sauce, Tabasco sauce, pickles and eggs. Pour into a ring mold, a rectangular pan, or individual custard cups. Chill. Serve on salad greens with mayonnaise on the side.

Pressed Chicken can be decorative if you slice the eggs instead of chopping them. Place a slice of egg in the bottom of each individual cup. Or arrange rows of sliced egg in the bottom of the loaf pan or in a circle around the ring mold. Then pour in the chicken mixture. When you serve the chicken on greens, the egg slices make an attractive garnish.

Preparing chicken like this may seem like a lot of trouble, but just think: Nowadays you can buy chicken already dressed. You only have to do the "pressing"! ❖

Stevan Dohanos

Delightful Desserts

Chapter Four

Mama looked rather defeated that day, and—frankly—my brother, sister and I had a lot to do with it. She had spent the rainy day putting up with roughhousing youngsters and was almost at the end of her rope.

I don't remember if there was some special occasion or if, as often was the case, she was simply trying to make supper special that evening. I do remember the cake she was lovingly mixing and baking.

I also remember vividly her admonishment to us as we stormed through the house.

"I'm about the put the cake in the oven," she said. "Don't run through the kitchen while it's baking, or you'll cause it to fall."

In those days, our simple home had only three rooms. The kitchen was centered between a living room and a bedroom, and it was the natural corridor for lawmen chasing rustlers or soldiers invading enemy lines.

Being the practical sort, I couldn't understand exactly how the galloping hooves of my trusty stick-horse could cause Mama's cake to fall.

After all, the cake was well-protected within the walls of the oven.

How could it fall out of there?

But, in addition to being practical, I also had an ornery side. So, when the charge

of the light brigade happened, it was me leading the way.

There was no noise from the oven, so I wrongly figured that all was quiet on the western front. The wail that followed was not an air raid siren, however. It was the anguished cry of a good cook gone mad.

In his Epistle to the Ephesians in the New Testament, the Apostle Paul talks about parents bringing their children up in the "nurture and the admonition of the Lord." Mama had always been really strong on the nurturing and usually left the admonition up to Daddy. Not on this day.

From that day on, I never had to be reminded to pull my steed up short when entering Mama's kitchen. It was a lot better for her cakes to leave a warm place in my heart rather than her hand leaving a warm place on my bottom.

And I never again caused the delapidation of one of her delightful desserts.

—Ken Tate

Pound Cake

This pound cake is one of Janice's delightful desserts that has been one of my favorites, and the source of a few extra pounds of my own! It is especially good served with freshly sliced strawberries and whipped cream.

Preheat oven to 350 degrees.

- 1 cup butter
- 1½ teaspoon vanilla
- 2 cups flour
- ¼ teaspoon nutmeg
- 2 cups sugar
- 6 eggs
- ¼ teaspoon salt

Cream butter, gradually adding sugar until light and fluffy. Add vanilla. Add eggs one at a time. Sift together flour, salt and nutmeg. Gradually add dry ingredients to egg mixture and beat until thoroughly blended. Turn batter into a greased bundt pan. Bake at 350 degrees for 40 minutes or until toothpick inserted into cake comes out clean.

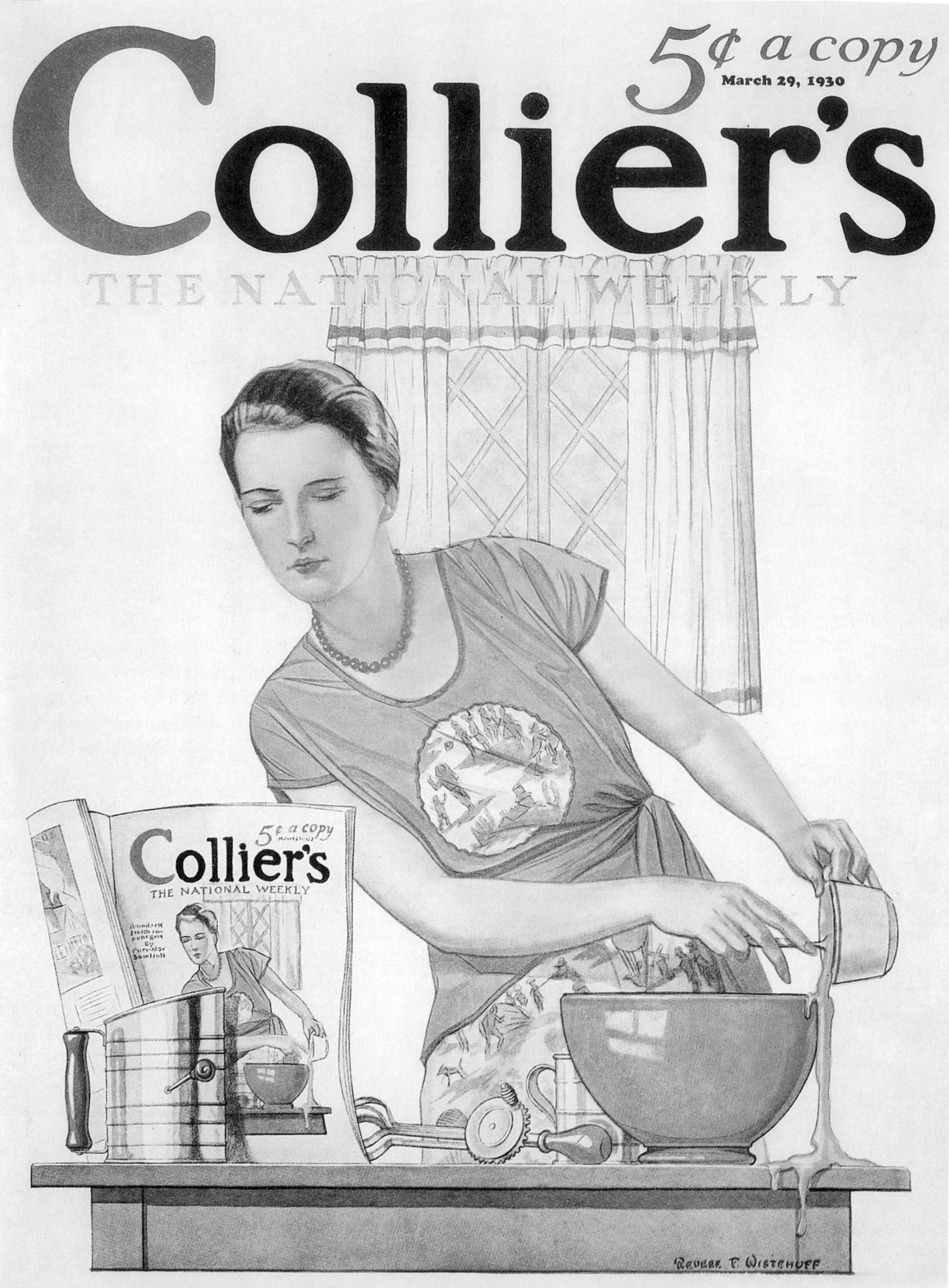

My First Angel Cake

By Bertie E. Burke

This is the story of my first angel cake, which I baked in a kettle. I was a young bride, 18 years old, and we had moved to a farm. I had done little cooking before I was married. I was the housekeeper and outside-tomboy type. I helped my mom in the garden and yard. My sister, a year younger than I, did the cooking.

That spring, my mother gave me 12 Barred Rock hens, plus one big rooster. These hens usually layed an egg a day—a big brown egg. I decided to bake an angel cake from a recipe in a cookbook my mother had given me a.

I had no real tube cake pan, so I decided to try baking it in a 1½-gallon kettle. It was 9 inches deep, with a metal bail. I did not have a wire whip for making the batter, so I used a fork. And my small range had no temperature gauge.

I carefully measured all the ingredients. I separated 12 of those eggs into a bowl, and mixed the batter as the recipe directed. The big batch of snowy batter looked beautiful to me.

One thing more: I had a tall jelly glass, which I placed in the center of the kettle. Then I carefully spooned the batter into the kettle around the glass. I handled the kettle with great care as I put it in the little wood stove's oven.

After an hour, I peeked in. To my amazement, there was a golden angel cake. I pressed it with my finger; it was ready to come from the oven. I turned the kettle upside down and let it cool.

I was so proud of myself! I had the most beautiful angel cake anyone ever saw. It came out of the kettle whole. I made white frosting for it, and it was the best cake I ever ate. After that ordeal, I decided that I could cook anything.

Later, I became the chief cook for the Woman's Club in St. Louis, Mo. That was my occupation until I was 50. Then I trained for nursing, and for 22 years, I nurtured the sick.

Now, I'm old, and my hands shake. But I'll never forget my first angel cake. ❖

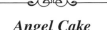

Angel Cake

1 cup cake flour
1½ cups sugar, divided
1¾ cups egg whites
¾ teaspoon salt
2 teaspoons cream of tartar
¾ cup sugar
1 teaspoon vanilla extract

Preheat oven to 325 degrees. Sift flour with ¾ cup sugar 4 times. Beat egg whites with salt until frothy; add cream of tartar and beat until stiff but not dry.

Add remaining ¾ cup sugar to egg whites, 1 tablespoon at a time, folding in thoroughly. Add vanilla extract with last addition of sugar. Sift flour mixture over the top of the batter a little at a time, and fold in carefully.

Spoon batter into a large, ungreased tube pan. Bake for 75 minutes. Invert pan to cool. The longer the cake remains in the pan, the more brown crust adheres to pan. Serves 16.

Angel Cake Variations

Chocolate Angel Cake: Substitute ¾ cup cake flour and 5 tablespoons cocoa powder for 1 cup cake flour. Sift cocoa with flour and ¾ cup sugar 4 times.

Holiday Angel Cake: Fold in ½ cup finely chopped, drained maraschino cherries just before baking. Frost with Seven-Minute Frosting and decorate as a Christmas, Valentine's Day, or Washington's Birthday cake.

Layered Angel Cake: Cut baked, cooled angel cake crosswise into 2 layers. Fold toasted almonds into flavored whipped cream; spread between cake layers. Frost with whipped cream and sprinkle generously with toasted, shredded almonds. Serve immediately.

Biblical Baking

By Charlene Wood

I t was sweet to eat, and a chance to modestly exhibit knowledge of the Bible. It was fun in the form of an early trivia game, and a great dish to take to a church supper. It was the scripture cake. No one knows where or when this cake was invented. It may have come from Europe or it may have been created along the Eastern Shore of early North America. We do know that it was spread by women.

As women moved across the country, the recipe went with them as a small, treasured bit from "back home." It usually traveled along as part of a prized collection of "receipts."

"Receipt" collections might include home remedies, housekeeping hints, and recipes for favorite dishes. Occasionally they contained a few bits of somewhat acerbic philosophy, such as that written by an unknown spokeswoman in a book titled *Cooking of the West*: "I declare that the woman who is able to systemize and carry on smoothly the

Managing editor Barb Sprunger used the Scripture Cake recipe to make this tempting dessert. House of White Birches photograph.

work of an ordinary family illustrates higher sagacity than is called for by seven-eighths of the tasks done by man. Men take one trade and work at it; a mother's and housekeeper's work requires a touch from all trades. Yes, a man's work brings in the money, but a man's work does not so tax the head and hands as a woman's work does."

But whether it included philosophies or recipes, the collection of "receipts" was a vital part of a woman's effort to establish and maintain a new home in a new country.

Follow Solomon's advice for making good boys: Proverbs 23:14.

When women moved West, the Bible was invariably one of the few books brought along. The Bible and the lady's "receipts" came side by side. They may have been the only reading material in many new homes. The scripture cake combines both of these literary sources.

This historical cake can still be made today. To play the game as our grandmothers might have played it, read the biblical list of ingredients and then write down your best guess as to what the ingredients actually are. Then, to be on the safe side, look in a King James Version of the Bible to verify your answers. You are now ready to make the cake and do your share in continuing a historical, friendly tradition.

If you wish to double-check your ingredients, a second, more conventional recipe is given here following the scriptural version. Good luck, and good eating.

Scripture Cake

1½ cups Judges 5:25
3 cups Jeremiah 6:20
6 Jeremiah 17:11
3½ cups Exodus 29:2
2 teaspoons Amos 4:5
II Chronicles 9:9 to taste
A pinch of Mark 9:50
1 cup Genesis 24:17

1 tablespoon I Samuel 14:25
2 cups I Samuel 30:12
2 cups chopped dried Song
    of Solomon 2:13
2 cups slivered or chopped
    Numbers 17:8

Follow Solomon's advice for making good boys: Proverbs 23:14.

Scripture Cake
Traditional Recipe

1½ cups butter
3 cups sugar
6 eggs
3½ cups flour
2 teaspoons baking powder
½ teaspoon ground nutmeg
1 teaspoon ground cloves
2 teaspoons cinnamon
1 teaspoon allspice
A pinch of salt
1 cup water
1 tablespoon honey
2 cups raisins
2 cups chopped dried figs
2 cups slivered or chopped almonds

Preheat oven to 325 degrees. Grease 2 (9 x 5 x 3-inch) loaf pans well.

Cream together butter and sugar. Beat in eggs one at a time, beating well after each addition. Sift together flour, baking powder, spices and salt. Add to creamed mixture alternately with water. Stir in honey. Fold in raisins, figs and almonds. Mix well.

Divide batter between prepared loaf pans. Bake for about 60 minutes, until loaves test done with the toothpick test. Do not overbake. Let cakes cool in pans for 30 minutes before turning out onto rack. Cool completely.

The winner of the scripture cake game can now enjoy the holy cake wholly! ❖

Delicious Desserts

*A*nyone will tell you that a meal is not complete until the dessert is served. The scrumptious delicacies that follow are the kind that almost make you gain weight by looking at them! So, moderation is the key as you head for the kitchen, heat up the oven and try out some of these delicious desserts. *Bon appetit!* ❖

Coffee Cloud Sponge Cake
The following recipe is from a 1955 advertisement announcing Mrs. John Matyola of Manville, N.J., as Best-of-Class Winner in Pillsbury's 6th Grand National Recipe and Baking Contest.

1 tablespoon instant coffee (see Note)
1 cup boiling water
2 cups sifted flour
3 teaspoons baking powder
½ teaspoon salt
6 eggs, separated
½ teaspoon cream of tartar
2 cups sugar, divided
1 teaspoon vanilla
1 cup pecans or other nuts, finely ground
Chopped nuts for garnish

Coffee Icing
2 tablespoons butter
2 cups sifted confectioners' sugar
1½ teaspoons instant coffee
2 tablespoons plus 2 or 3 teaspoons milk

For cake, dissolve instant coffee in boiling water; cool. **Note:** *1 cup cold, double-strength brewed coffee may be substituted for the instant coffee and boiling water.*

Preheat oven to 350 degrees. Sift together sifted flour, baking powder and salt.

Beat egg whites (about ¾ cup) with cream of tartar in a large bowl until very soft mounds begin to form. Add ½ cup sugar to egg whites 2 tablespoons at a time; continue beating until very stiff, straight peaks form when beater is raised. Do not underbeat. Set aside.

Beat egg yolks (about ½ cup) in large mixer bowl until blended; gradually add 1½ cups sugar and vanilla. Beat at high speed until thick and lemon-colored, 4 to 5 minutes.

Facing page: 1935 Baker's Chocolate ad, House of White Birches nostalgia archives

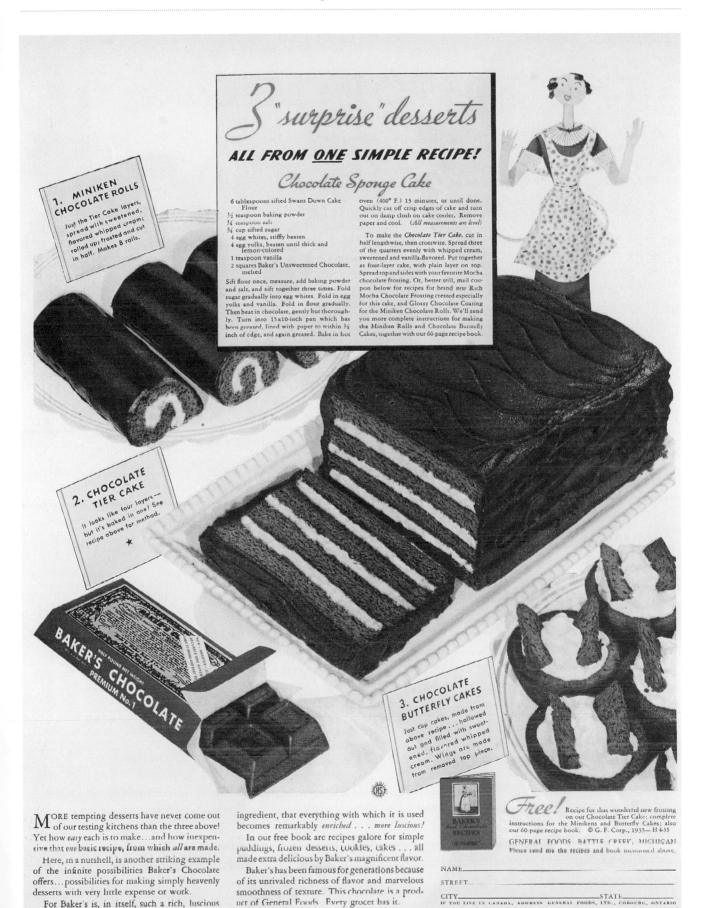

3 "surprise" desserts

ALL FROM ONE SIMPLE RECIPE!

Chocolate Sponge Cake

6 tablespoons sifted Swans Down Cake Flour
½ teaspoon baking powder
¼ teaspoon salt
¾ cup sifted sugar
4 egg whites, stiffly beaten
4 egg yolks, beaten until thick and lemon-colored
1 teaspoon vanilla
2 squares Baker's Unsweetened Chocolate, melted

Sift flour once, measure, add baking powder and salt, and sift together three times. Fold sugar gradually into egg whites. Fold in egg yolks and vanilla. Fold in flour gradually. Then beat in chocolate, gently but thoroughly. Turn into 15x10-inch pan which has been greased, lined with paper to within ¼ inch of edge, and again greased. Bake in hot oven (400° F.) 13 minutes, or until done. Quickly cut off crisp edges of cake and turn out on damp cloth on cake cooler. Remove paper and cool. *(All measurements are level)*

To make the *Chocolate Tier Cake*, cut in half lengthwise, then crosswise. Spread three of the quarters evenly with whipped cream, sweetened and vanilla-flavored. Put together as four-layer cake, with plain layer on top. Spread top and sides with your favorite Mocha chocolate frosting. Or, better still, mail coupon below for recipes for brand *new* Rich Mocha Chocolate Frosting created especially for this cake, and Glossy Chocolate Coating for the Miniken Chocolate Rolls. We'll send you more complete instructions for making the Miniken Rolls and Chocolate Butterfly Cakes, together with our 60-page recipe book.

1. MINIKEN CHOCOLATE ROLLS
Just the Tier Cake layers, spread with sweetened, flavored whipped cream; rolled up, frosted and cut in half. Makes 8 rolls.

2. CHOCOLATE TIER CAKE
It looks like four layers — but it's baked in one! See recipe above for method.

3. CHOCOLATE BUTTERFLY CAKES
Just cup cakes, made from above recipe . . . hollowed out and filled with sweetened, flavored whipped cream. Wings are made from removed top piece.

BAKER'S CHOCOLATE
PREMIUM No. 1

BAKER'S Best Chocolate RECIPES

Free! Recipe for that wonderful new frosting on our Chocolate Tier Cake; complete instructions for the Minikens and Butterfly Cakes; also our 60-page recipe book. © G. F. Corp., 1935—H 4-35

GENERAL FOODS, BATTLE CREEK, MICHIGAN
Please send me the recipes and book mentioned above.

NAME_____

STREET_____

CITY_____STATE_____
IF YOU LIVE IN CANADA, ADDRESS GENERAL FOODS, LTD., COBOURG, ONTARIO

MORE tempting desserts have never come out of our testing kitchens than the three above! Yet how *easy* each is to make . . . and how inexpensive that *one basic recipe*, from which *all* are made.

Here, in a nutshell, is another striking example of the infinite possibilities Baker's Chocolate offers . . . possibilities for making simply heavenly desserts with very little expense or work.

For Baker's is, in itself, such a rich, luscious ingredient, that everything with which it is used becomes remarkably *enriched . . . more luscious!*

In our free book are recipes galore for simple puddings, frozen desserts, cookies, cakes . . . all made extra delicious by Baker's magnificent flavor.

Baker's has been famous for generations because of its unrivaled richness of flavor and marvelous smoothness of texture. This chocolate is a product of General Foods. Every grocer has it.

Add the dry ingredients alternately with cooled coffee to egg-yolk mixture, beginning and ending with dry ingredients. Blend thoroughly after each addition. (With electric mixer, use a low speed.)

Fold in finely ground nuts by hand; blend thoroughly. Fold egg-yolk mixture, ¼ at a time, into the stiffly beaten egg whites by hand. Fold only 15 strokes after each addition, using a wire whip or spatula. After last addition, continue folding just until evenly blended.

Pour batter into ungreased 10-inch tube pan. Bake for 60 to 70 minutes. Invert immediately; cool in pan for at least 1 hour. Frost with coffee icing and sprinkle top with additional chopped nuts, if desired.

For icing, cream butter. Blend in confectioners' sugar and instant coffee, creaming well. Gradually add milk until of spreading consistency.

1936 Gold Medal Flour ad, House of White Birches nostalgia archives

Orange Slice Cake

1 pound candy orange slices, chopped
½ pound candied pineapple
2 cups sweetened, flaked coconut
2 cups pecans, chopped
3½ cups flour, divided
1 cup butter
3 cups sugar, divided
4 eggs
2 teaspoons grated orange rind
1 teaspoon baking soda
1 cup buttermilk
½ cup orange juice
Orange liqueur to taste (optional)

Preheat oven to 300 degrees. Butter and flour a tube or bundt pan, or 4 loaf pans. (Nonstick pans work best.)

Mix candy orange slices, pineapple, coconut, and pecans in 1 cup of flour. Set aside. Cream butter and 2 cups sugar until fluffy. Add eggs one at a time, beating well after each addition. Blend in orange rind.

Mix together baking soda and 2½ cups flour. Add flour mixture alternately with buttermilk to creamed mixture. Mix well. Stir in candy mixture. Pour into pan of choice and bake until wooden pick inserted in cake comes out clean. The time will vary, depending on the size of the pan. Baking will take almost 2 hours for the bundt pan.

Mix orange juice and 1 cup sugar in a small saucepan. Bring to boil. Blend in orange liqueur to taste. While hot cake is still in pan, poke holes in cake and pour boiling orange juice mixture over top. Turn cake out of pan; brush orange juice mixture over sides and top of cake with a pastry brush. Let cool.

Enchanted Cream Sponge
This recipe is for the cake featured in the 1936 Swans Down Cake Flour ad at the bottom of facing page.

1 cup sifted cake flour
1 teaspoon baking powder
¼ teaspoon salt
2 eggs, separated
½ cup cold water

1 teaspoon grated lemon rind
¾ cup plus 2 tablespoons sugar,
    divided
1 teaspoon lemon juice

Lemon Cream Filling & Sauce
1 cup sugar
5 tablespoons cake flour
1 egg, lightly beaten
⅓ cup lemon juice
⅔ cup water
2 teaspoons butter
1 teaspoon grated lemon rind
1 cup whipped cream, divided

Preheat oven to 350 degrees. For cake, mix sifted flour with baking powder and salt; sift together three times.

Combine egg yolks, water and lemon rind, and beat with rotary eggbeater until light and foamy. Gradually add ¾ cup sugar, beating well after each addition.

Add sifted dry ingredients in small amounts, beating with beater enough to blend.

Beat egg whites until foamy throughout. Add lemon juice and 2 tablespoons sugar; beat until stiff enough to stand up in peaks. Fold into flour mixture. Turn batter into two ungreased deep 8-inch round pans. Bake for 25 minutes, or until done. Invert on rack until cakes are cold.

For Lemon Cream Filling, combine sugar and cake flour in top of double boiler. Add egg, lemon juice, water and butter, mixing thoroughly. Place over boiling water and cook for 10 minutes, stirring constantly. Chill. Fold in grated lemon rind and ¼ cup whipped cream. Spread half the filling between the cooled cake layers. Sprinkle top of cake with confectioners' sugar.

For Lemon Cream Sauce, fold ¾ cup whipped cream into the remaining filling. Serve sauce with slices of cake.

Georgia Pecan Pie

Pastry for 8-inch single-crust pie
3 eggs, beaten
¾ cup molasses
¾ cup light corn syrup
½ cup strong brewed coffee
2 tablespoons butter, melted
1 teaspoon salt
1 teaspoon vanilla
1 cup chopped pecans
¼ cup sifted flour

Line pie plate with pastry, crimping rim into a decorative edge. Preheat oven to 375 degrees. Combine eggs, molasses, corn syrup, coffee, butter, salt and vanilla. Mix thoroughly. Combine pecans and flour. Add to egg mixture. Stir to mix well. Pour into unbaked pie shell. Bake 40 to 45 minutes, until firm. Let cool to room temperature before cutting. Serves 6 to 8.

—*Edith Wright Holmes*

Cherry Puff

2½ cups tart cherries, drained (½ cup juice reserved)
½ cup plus ⅓ cup sugar, divided
2 tablespoons quick-cooking tapioca
2 egg whites
Dash of salt
¼ teaspoon cream of tartar
2 egg yolks
6 tablespoons cake flour

Preheat oven to 325 degrees. Crush cherries with potato masher in a saucepan; add reserved cherry juice, ½ cup sugar and tapioca. Simmer for 5 minutes, stirring constantly. Set aside.

Beat egg whites until foamy; add salt and cream of tartar; beat until stiff. Beat egg yolks until thick and lemon-colored; add ⅓ cup sugar; beat thoroughly. Fold egg yolks into egg whites, then fold in cake flour. Pour cherry mixture in to 1½–quart casserole. Pour batter on top. Bake for 40 minutes. Serve warm. Serves 6.

—*Edith Wright Holmes*

Papa's Homestead Cake

By Marvel Stephen

Tucked inside the birthday card were a recipe and a note from a thoughtful cousin explaining that my father had given this cake recipe to her mother when they were living on adjoining homesteads in western Montana. This was before my father and mother were married, so the year must have been about 1918. ❖

Papa's Homestead Cake

1 cup sugar
1 cup raisins
1 cup hot water, plus extra
    or dissolving baking soda
½ cup shortening
2 heaping tablespoons cocoa
1 teaspoon cinnamon
½ teaspoon nutmeg
½ teaspoon ground allspice
¼ teaspoon ground ginger
1 scant teaspoon baking soda
2 eggs, beaten
1½ cups sifted flour
½ teaspoon salt
1 cup chopped walnuts

Combine sugar, raisins, 1 cup hot water, shortening, cocoa and spices in a heavy saucepan. Bring to a boil and boil for 3 minutes. Cool.

Preheat oven to 350 degrees. Grease a 9 x 9-inch baking pan. To cooked, cooled mixture, add baking soda mixed with a little hot water. Blend in eggs. Sift together flour and salt; add to mixture. Stir in walnuts.

Pour batter into prepared pan and bake for 35 to 45 minutes, or until cake tests done.

Grandma Dillard's Apple Cake

By Doretha Dillard Shipman

*M*y mother baked this apple cake when I was growing up in the hills of north Arkansas in the 1930s. It was *so* good and moist! "The applesauce makes it that way," she'd say, The leftovers stayed fresh for a while—that is, if there *were* any.

I think back to our old kitchen/ dining room with the Home Comfort woodstove, the homemade meal and flour bin, and the cistern on the back porch next to the kitchen door.

Neither icebox nor refrigerator was anywhere to be seen. Mom sometimes would swing the lard bucket of milk in the cistern to cool it for our supper in the summertime, hoping it would not spill.

The porches on those old homes always had a shelf built between the posts to hold buckets of cream waiting to be churned, and clabber milk or buttermilk waiting to be poured into biscuits or corn bread.

Mom loved to cook with plenty of butter. She had learned some of her cooking from her mother-in-law, my grandmother, Nancy Smith Dillard. Grandmother always tried to have good, fresh butter, especially for breakfast. Mother also wanted, above all, to have butter for breakfast. Sometimes this meant doing without it for dinner or supper. Housewives back then learned to manage.

Grandmother had so many children and so much company; I heard my folks say that Grandma sometimes had to pour water into the milk to have enough to go around.

We were all happy when Grandma baked her stacked applesauce cake. It is a very old recipe. She taught her daughters how to make it, and now we granddaughters and great-granddaughters make it.

I am glad for my heritage. I am thankful for my grandmother, mom and aunts, from whom I learned so much. This is how we remembered the recipe for Grandma's apple cake in our Dillard family cookbook, *Home Cookin'*. ❖

Grandma Dillard's Apple Cake

3¼ cups sugar, divided
1½ cups shortening
3 eggs
Pinch of salt
1 cup buttermilk
4 cups flour

1 teaspoon baking soda
1 teaspoon baking powder
2 teaspoons vanilla
2 pints applesauce

Preheat oven to 350 degrees. For cake, cream 2½ cups sugar with shortening. Add eggs, baking soda, salt and baking powder; add buttermilk and vanilla. Sift in flour and mix until very stiff.

Toss a small amount of dough on the dough board and roll out as for cookies; cut with an 8-inch plate. Continue until all dough is used. Bake on large cookie sheet. Makes 13–14 "cookies."

Meanwhile, for filling, heat applesauce; add ¾ cup sugar (more or less to taste). On a large plate, alternate cookies with applesauce until all are used.

Mama's Fruitcake

By Ruth Kirkpatrick Townsend

One of the nicest memories from my childhood is Mama's fruitcake and how it was made in the kitchen and aged in the parlor. Mama used a recipe that had been handed down to her by her mother. It had been in the family for years. It had grape jelly in it, and chocolate, too, if you can imagine such a combination. Some of the instructions weren't very exact, and the recipe just said to put in spices to taste. Mama finally wrote down the main ingredients pretty definitely, but she always just shook in the cinnamon and nutmeg and such. You'll find the recipe at the end so you can try it if you want to, and I hope you will want to.

When Mama got ready to make fruitcake, she always took down the big dishpan from where it hung on the wall of the entryway. Every time she would say, "We need something big and this is the best thing we have." Mama would wash the dishpan well and set it on the kitchen table.

My sister and I always got busy then, cutting up the dates and nuts and setting out the candied fruit and citron and raisins and currants.

There's nothing better to bring the joy of Christmas into your home.

Mama used homemade butter. She put it in the dishpan and made sure it was good and soft. If it wasn't just right, she took a spoon and chopped at it until it suited her. Then she mixed in the brown sugar. After that came the beaten eggs and the soda dissolved in the hot water. Then she added the flour and the spices.

After all that was mixed in, my sister and I got to put in the fruits and nuts. We each got to take a turn, trying to stir the mixture, but usually we just weren't strong enough to do it the way Mama wanted. She held the dishpan up against her stomach and stirred vigorously. Then she stopped to grate a couple of squares of chocolate. The chocolate kind of fluffed up as she grated it so two squares were enough usually to fill 3 tablespoons. Once in recent years I tried using that soft, runny chocolate you get in little plastic envelopes and it was terrible. It made the cakes look all grayish. It didn't hurt the taste, as far as we could see, but it sure wasn't good to look at.

After the chocolate, she put in the jelly. It was always homemade jelly (though "boughten" works OK). We loved to look at it and smelled of the ripe grapes we had picked under the late summer sun.

For baking, the batter was put in waxed-paper–lined bread pans. Mama made sure the fire in the big cookstove had died down properly. Fruitcake had to cook slowly. Nowadays I use my electric stove, of course, but it never seems quite as much fun as when Mama used her old black stove with the big chunks of firewood standing by and the basket of cobs handy in case the oven began to cool off too much.

After the cakes came out of the oven, they were set aside to cool completely. Then Mama peeled off the waxed paper very carefully. After that, each loaf had to be wrapped in a fresh piece of waxed paper and finally covered entirely with a clean dish towel. Then all the cakes were packed in an old airtight metal bread box to mellow. The bread box stood on a table in the northwest corner of the cool, dark parlor.

1947 Jane Parker Fruitcake ad, House of White Birches nostalgia archives

Cakes were supposed to age for many months, even a year sometimes. I don't think I've ever stored mine more than a week or two. I just don't get at it until right before Christmas, but I think it tastes just as good, and you don't have to worry about mold (though Mama never seemed to have any trouble).

When Christmastime finally arrived, Mama would go into the parlor to open the bread box. My sister and I would tag along. We loved the delicious smell of the fruits and nuts when she opened the lid. Mama let one of us carry the chosen cake out into the dining room.

With bated breath we watched Mama unwrap it. She took her sharpest knife and cut some thin, very thin, slices. Mama always said,

"Fruitcake is rich, you know, and little girls can't have too much," so my sister and I would share a slice.

Papa got a big piece. He always said he married Mama so he could have her fruitcake every Christmas. We laughed at his little joke and then sat down to enjoy our piece of cake.

Modern boughten fruitcakes are good and I like them, but for true Christmas joy, try making Mama's fruitcake for your family, just once at least. There's nothing better to bring the joy of Christmas into your home. ❖

Mama's Fruitcake

2 cups butter or margarine, softened
2½ cups brown sugar
7 beaten eggs
1 teaspoon baking soda dissolved
      in 2 tablespoons hot water
4 cups flour
½–1 teaspoon ground cinnamon
½–1 teaspoon ground nutmeg
Other spices to taste
1 pound raisins
1 pound currants
1 pound dates
½ pound citron
1 cup chopped nuts
2 cups candied fruits, or more to taste
3 tablespoons grated chocolate
½ cup grape jelly

Into softened butter, blend brown sugar, then eggs, then dissolved baking soda, blending thoroughly after each addition. Stir in flour and spices; mix well. Stir in fruits and nuts, blending well. Mix in grated chocolate, blending thoroughly. Blend in jelly, mixing well.

Line greased bread pans with waxed paper; divide fruitcake batter among prepared pans. Bake in a 275- or 300-degree oven for 1 hour, or until done.

Set pans on rack to cool. When cool, carefully peel off waxed paper. Wrap each loaf in fresh waxed paper, and then in a clean dish towel or cheesecloth. Set aside in a cool, dark place for at least a week to allow fruitcakes to mellow.

Joy of Ice Cream

By Esther Coffield

When winter's first blustery winds blew through the cracks of our small southern Ohio home, one of the first chores was to stuff catalog pages into the gaps. Shortly thereafter, our thoughts turned to ice-cream making. After all, the only time we could make ice cream was when the nearby creek was frozen solid.

Then, seven siblings in stair-step sizes, bundled up to our noses, pulled a sled over the frozen ground, down to the creek. With a small ax we chopped chunks of ice to load onto the sled. The rustic, oak-planked ice-cream bucket stood ready and waiting on the front porch.

In the shadow of snowcapped hills, we trudged through the snow to the shed where Pansy the cow lived. One of us would carry the galvanized bucket and place the three-legged stool in position. Then we took turns relieving Pansy of her burden of warm milk.

When the milk had cooled, Mother skimmed rich cream from the top. We gathered fresh eggs from the nests of squawking hens. Then all the precious ingredients came together in a large black kettle on top of the woodstove.

We'd no longer have to wait for the creek to freeze.

Mother didn't need a recipe—just memories passed down from her mother, which probably had come from her mother's mother. One chore that we didn't complain about was cranking the handle. When the crank became difficult to turn, we knew that the special treat was almost ready to gobble up.

As the Great Depression years gave way to World War II, it was time to leave our home in the backwoods so that Dad could find work to feed his hungry brood. The old 1937 Plymouth was loaded down with all our worldly goods, including crates filled with squawking chickens and, of course, the cherished ice-cream maker. At the time we didn't realize that we'd no longer have to wait for the creek to freeze to enjoy our favorite treat.

Our new house, closer to civilization, was actually quite old, with floodwater marks halfway up the walls. But now we had the luxury of an icebox. The iceman delivered twice a week, sinking tongs into a block of ice that he hefted onto his shoulder, thoroughly soaking his blue shirt. We kids gathered at the back of the truck, sneaking small pieces of ice to chew. Simple pleasures!

With ice at the ready, we could now make ice cream anytime there was enough money to buy the ingredients. We'd had to leave Pansy behind in the hills with a deserving family. Even so, we savored the wonderfully delicious treat made with store-bought groceries. Now we realized that most of the flavor resulted from Mother's loving touch.

Again we moved up in the world.

Our next house, closer to the city, had indoor plumbing and an electric icebox. Mother sometimes sent us to the small corner grocery to buy one pint of Neapolitan ice cream to be divided among our family of nine.

The mom-and-pop store-owners were baffled when we asked for a "poke" for the ice cream, until they determined that we needed a sack.

But the store-bought variety was no equal to our homemade ice cream!

Now old enough to baby-sit, I was able occasionally to visit the corner drugstore soda fountain.

I'd stare, transfixed, at the menu on the wall behind the Formica counter.

Which flavor to choose—vanilla, chocolate, strawberry? What tough decisions there were to make in life!

In just a few years I had children of my own. On birthdays and special occasions they could request favorite flavors to be churned in a new, electric ice-cream maker. At family gatherings, my siblings and I reminisced about the old times and making our favorite dessert.

I also introduced ice-cream making to my precious grandchildren, who enjoy watching the magical contraption revolve as they help by adding the salt and ice. As the freezer slows, they know that bowls will soon be piled high with a yummy treat. The love of ice cream definitely runs in our family!

As I ponder changed times, from chopping ice in winter and gathering eggs in apron pockets to modern conveniences, I find that the Depression years have faded into the recesses of my memory. Even though our precious mother has passed on, her cherished legacies remain in our hearts.

Nestled among those memories is the wonderfully delicious, old-fashioned, homemade custard ice cream, made with loving hands and served to her large brood. We've never been able to duplicate the recipe that we enjoyed back home in the hills. ❖

Old-Fashioned Vanilla Ice Cream
(6-quart freezer)

3½ cups sugar
¾ teaspoon salt
6 eggs, beaten
2 tablespoons vanilla
½ cup flour
7 cups milk
6 cups whipping cream

Combine sugar, flour and salt in large saucepan. Gradually stir in milk; cook over medium heat for approximately 15 minutes, or until thickened, stirring constantly.

Gradually stir about 1 cup of hot mixture into beaten eggs. Add eggs to remaining hot mixture, stirring constantly. Cook for 1 minute. Remove from heat. Let cool, then refrigerate for about 2 hours. Combine whipping cream and vanilla and add to chilled mixture, stirring with wire whisk. Freeze according to ice-cream maker's directions.

Designer Ice Creams

By Helen Brassel

esigner ice creams are ice creams that can be made with your own personal touches put right into them. Because these ice creams are so uncomplicated, it's easy to change them around to suit your own particular preference. The vanilla ice creams, for example, would be delightful with the additions of your favorite fruit or cookies. Add maraschino cherries to chocolate ice cream or substitute raspberry syrup for the Grand Marnier in Chocolate Mousse Ice Cream.

Powdered flavorings and concentrated extracts can do the same thing. Add cinnamon and you have Spanish chocolate; add almond extract for Viennese chocolate; and add coffee to get a mocha flavor.

Although there is very little effort involved in the making of these ice creams, the finished products are rich, smooth and creamy.

The finished products are rich, smooth and creamy.

Freezing in a shallow dish speeds the process along, and covering the tray with waxed paper helps prevent the formation of ice crystals.

A lot has happened to ice cream in the long migration from homemade to supermarket. There are more than 1,200 flavorings, colors, stabilizers and emulsifiers available to the commercial producer of ice cream.

The old-time ice-cream makers dealt primarily with cream, sugar and various flavorings. So can you, using the recipes below and on the following pages. ❖

Butter Pecan Ice Cream

1 package cook-and-serve
    butterscotch pudding mix
1½ cups heavy cream
¾ cup strong coffee
½ cup light corn syrup
1 teaspoon vanilla
1 cup heavy cream, whipped
¾ cup pecan halves

Combine pudding mix, heavy cream and coffee. Cook over medium heat until thickened. Add corn syrup and vanilla. Fold in whipped cream and pecans. Cover and freeze. Serves 8.

Supper Around the Table

Chapter Five

"Honey! I'm home!" I probably sounded a little like Desi Arnaz greeting Lucille Ball on the old *I Love Lucy* television show back when we were first married. It only seemed natural. Janice's beautiful red hair would rival Lucy's, even if I were never quite handsome enough or Latin enough to pass for Ricky Ricardo.

The similarities probably didn't end there, either. While Janice was ready to give me that welcome-home kiss I was probably, more often than not, focused on the question that has haunted men for ages: "What's for supper?" I never was very good at multitasking, but I sure was able to accept that smooch while uncovering the delicacies Janice was preparing for the kids and me.

Supper for us was a continuation of the rituals of life. After cleaning up a bit, I joined the rest of the family. We all gathered around the kitchen table that Janice had generously laden with food fit for a king, a queen, a prince and a couple of princesses.

We bowed heads and gave thanks to a Beneficent Creator who had protected us through the day, who had provided for us and who had brought us together again for supper around the table.

Children were loaded down with excitement from the day's adventures to share with me. A hike to the bluff line down by the creek yielded a lizard that had to be the biggest they had ever seen. A surprise visit by Grandpa on his old Ford tractor ended with a short jaunt on his hay wagon. The barn cat had kittens. The stories usually began: "Papa, you wouldn't believe … !"

I have always been proud that "Just wait until your father gets home!" was not normally a call to disciplinary action.

It was simply Janice's way of corralling youthful exuberance.

What was for supper? Even though it grabbed my attention at the door, the food ultimately became secondary. It could be steak, macaroni or hamburger cheese bake (one of my favorite evening meals). All that really mattered was that I was home, surrounded by the love of my family as we enjoyed supper around the table in the Good Old Days.

—*Ken Tate*

> *The stories usually began:*
> *"Papa, you wouldn't believe … !"*

Ellen's Hamburger Cheese Bake

This recipe was given to Janice by her best friend, Ellen. It makes a great supper casserole.

Preheat oven to 350 degrees.
1 pound ¼- or ½-inch flat egg noodles, cooked and drained
1 pound hamburger, cooked and drained
24 ounces cottage cheese
8 ounces sour cream
Salt and pepper to taste

Place a layer of half of the cooked noodles in a 2-quart casserole dish. Next comes a layer of half of the cottage cheese. Then a layer of half of the cooked hamburger. Finally a layer of half of the sour cream. Repeat layers a second time to fill the dish. Cover and bake about 45 minutes or until bubbly. Makes 6 servings.

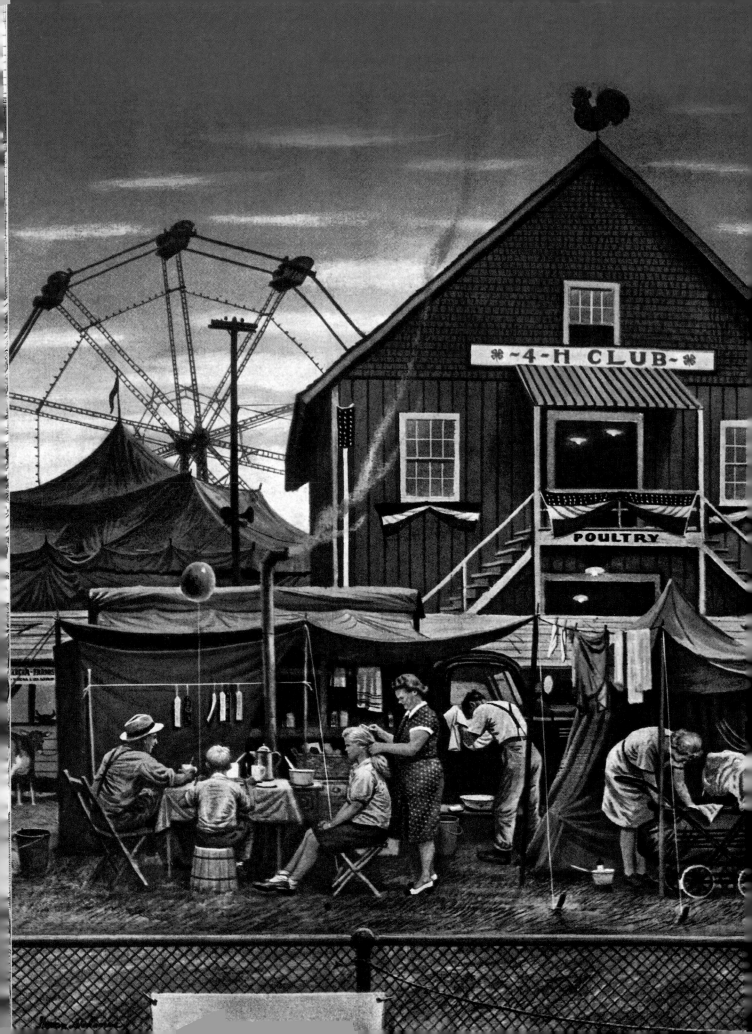

4-H in the 1950s

By Frances W. Muir

I was active in the 4-H organization for nine years, from the fourth grade in Nebraska back in 1950 until I graduated from high school in Delaware. 4-H, the largest such organization for young people in the country, grew out of the rural environment, but quickly became established in towns and cities as well. It is closely allied with the Agricultural Extension Service of local governments, which provides support and information to adults as well as groups such as the 4-H.

4-H was something I could do with Mama, who was happy to have someone else teach me to sew. She'd discovered that not only was it difficult to teach one's own child technical skills of this sort; but being a right-handed person, as she was, trying to teach a "lefty" like me, she was already doomed to frustration.

4-H involved regular meetings with a group leader. Learning activities were developed by the organization for us to complete. These

4-H taught me the most important basics of food and cooking.

activities could involve anything related to home and farm, but I worked entirely in the areas of cooking and sewing. We also promoted our group with occasional displays in local store windows.

Through such activities, we were able to achieve measured levels of accomplishment. 4-H taught me the most important basics about food and cooking, including:

- Serve simple food in generous amounts.
- Select a balanced menu, something from each food group.
- Choose a variety of textures, colors, flavor and temperatures.
- Always use top-quality ingredients.
- Prepare and cook each food to its proper consistency.
- When ready to eat, hot foods should be hot and cold foods cold.
- Garnish the food dishes and place on an attractively set table.

These simple guidelines aren't often mentioned in modern efforts to present more exotic food ideas, but following them ensures good nutrition, a nice presentation on the table, well-fed family and guests, and not too much work for the cook.

We almost always displayed our best handiwork at the annual county and state fairs. It was gratifying to receive ribbons and awards for the items I submitted. When I was in high school, these competitions culminated in my winning a division of the Delaware State 4-H Favorite Foods Contest at the local and then the state level.

Each contest was set up the same way. A large auditorium held rows of gas ranges, contributed by a local gas company, and a crew of gas-company employees stood by to make sure they were in good working order.

Work areas were set up in front of each range, along with a place to arrange a table setting, which was also part of what we were judged on.

Mama had helped me plan for the contest and had gotten a recipe for oven-fried chicken from a friend. It was simple but tasty.

We decided that I should compete in the lunch division. Mama and I devised a table setting using her best dinnerware, which was white with a broad maroon band around the edge.

I made a fringed place mat and matching napkin from a scrap of forest green fabric, and devised a centerpiece. I had to come up with a complete menu, and I chose broccoli and home-made yeast rolls to go with the chicken.

By the time the actual contest began, I was well-rehearsed. I had no problem, except that the crumbs managed to get scattered around a lot. About the only negative comment from the judges was "Could be neater."

It was gratifying to win the award, but even more satisfying to find that the gas-company employees liked the chicken so much that mine was the first dish they finished off after the competition.

At the state competition, when the awards were announced, someone else's name was read for third place and then second.

I wasn't particularly concerned about winning; just getting into the state contest was pretty good, as far as I was concerned.

Mama told me later that she really wanted me to win something, as she was afraid that I'd be disappointed if I didn't.

So when my name was called for first

Head, heart, hands and health—the 4-H motto is: "To make the best better." A schoolgirl demonstrates better cooking methods at the 4-H spring fair in Adrian, Ore., in May 1941. Photograph courtesy the FSA-OWI Collection and the Library of Congress.

place, she was even more thrilled than I was. I posed with the other winners for newspaper pictures and I treasured the award platter I own, which is still displayed prominently in my home. ❖

Frances' Winning Oven-Fried Chicken

Chicken pieces, skin removed
Ritz crackers
⅓ cup butter
Paprika

Preheat oven to 350 degrees. In the meantime, wash and dry chicken pieces. Use a rolling pin to crush the crackers between two layers of clean cloth (or, these days, crumble in a food processor).

Melt the butter in a baking pan, turning the pan to coat the bottom and sides evenly. Place the chicken in the pan and turn the pieces to coat evenly with butter. Coat each piece of chicken thoroughly with the crushed crackers and return to buttered pan. Scatter extra crumbs over top and sprinkle with paprika.

Bake for 30 minutes, or until juices run clear when chicken is pierced with a fork. Serve with broccoli, rolls with butter, and a cold gelatin salad.